Living
Without Limitations

30 MENTORS
TO ROCK YOUR WORLD!

•

Compiled by
ANITA SECHESKY

Published by Marketing for Coach, Ltd
Second Floor
6th London Street
W2 1HR London (UK)

www.coachingandsuccess.com
info@coachingandsuccess.com

ISBN: 978-0-9575561-4-0

Published in UK, Europe, US and Canada

Book Cover: Csernik Előd

Inside Layout: Csernik Előd

To Victoria!

Live Without

Limitations

A Secks J

Table of Contents

Legal Disclaimer. 1

Foreword 3

With Love and Gratitude 5

Introduction 9

CHAPTER 1
Discovering Your Life Without Limitations
Anita Sechesky. 14

CHAPTER 2
**Embracing Your Birth Given Right
to Unlimited Abundance**
Hanna Hashim. 20

CHAPTER 3
In Search Of True Happiness
Sandi Chomyn 26

CHAPTER 4
In Pursuit of Passion! Individual, Relational and Intimate
Kristy-Lea Tritz 32

CHAPTER 5
Answering Destiny's Call
Holly Osler Bartsch 38

CHAPTER 6
Break the Blocks to Business Success!
W. A. Read Knox 44

CHAPTER 7
What in the World Are You Doing After Retirement?
Gwendolyn Weir Swint 50

CHAPTER 8
Reframe Your Marketing Mindset
Pat Campbell 56

CHAPTER 9
Inspire Your Ambition
Viviana Andrew 62

CHAPTER 10
How To Be Organized for Success
Patrick Hayden 68

CHAPTER 11
Unshakable You
Stacey Cargnelutti 74

CHAPTER 12
**Mind Map Your Vision with Passion and Power:
Creating Clarity Out of Confusion**
Leta Russell 82

CHAPTER 13
Balancing Life – Keep the Wheels of Life Turning
Mike Gillespie 88

CHAPTER 14
**Change is Gonna Come: Stop Dreading
and Start Harnessing Its Power!**
Michael Hanle 94

CHAPTER 15
**Dealing with Prickly
Personalities**
Krista VonWiller 100

CHAPTER 16
**Transforming the Energy of your
Subconscious Programming**
Shannon Staples. 106

CHAPTER 17
Expose and Empower Your Gifts and Talents
Rebecca David 112

CHAPTER 18
Out of Your Mind and Into Your Heart
Mental and Emotional Mastery
Hazel Moore 118

CHAPTER 19
Money Mastery is Your Key to Prosperity
Faith Dugan 124

CHAPTER 20
Cranking it Up! – Living your life out LOUD!
Stephen Yuzenko 130

CHAPTER 21
The Law of Appreciation: The Sacred Whispering
of Your Heart
Subira Folami 136

CHAPTER 22
Blend Clarity and Focus for a More Effective
and Peaceful You
Donna Apilado-Schumacher 142

CHAPTER 23
The True Value of Stress;
From Overwhelmed to Overjoyed
Teresa Mason Maron 148

CHAPTER 24
Breaking through the Bondage of Bullying
Jan Robberts 156

CHAPTER 25
Shift Out of your Self-Destructive Cycle
Warren Broad 162

CHAPTER 26
Productivity for Creative Procrastinators
Beverly Garland 168

CHAPTER 27
Cultivating Self-Confidence, One Seed at a Time
Elizabeth Pennington. 174

CHAPTER 28
Your Unique Leader's Voice.
A Journey Through Trauma
Carol Metz Murray 180

CHAPTER 29
Finding Your Path to Awesome: Break Free
and Live the Adventure
Peter Frumenti. 186

CHAPTER 30
LOVE … It's What You're Waiting For!
Anita Sechesky. 192

Endorsement. 197

Afterword 199

Legal Disclaimer

The information and content contained within this book, "Living Without Limitations – 30 Mentors to Rock your World!" is not a substitute for any form of professional counsel such as a Psychologist, Physician or Counselor. The contents and information provided do not constitute professional or legal advice in any way, shape or form.

Any decisions you make and the outcomes thereof are entirely your own doing. Under no circumstances can you hold the Author or "Anita Sechesky – Living Without Limitations" liable for any actions that you take.

You agree not to hold the Author or "Anita Sechesky – Living Without Limitations" liable for any loss or expense incurred by you, as a result of materials, advice, coaching or mentoring offered within.

The information offered in this book is intended to be general information with respect to general life issues. Information is offered in good faith; however you are under no obligation to use this information.

Nothing contained in this book shall be considered legal, financial, or actuarial advice.

Information in this book is written to introduce what a Life Coach, Counselor or Therapist may discuss with you at any given time during scheduled sessions. It is not meant, however, to replace the Professional roles of these individuals.

Living *Without* **Limitations**

Foreword

Many of the boundaries that slow down or even halt our ability to achieve goals are self-imposed. But it sure doesn't seem that way when the goals are yours. It can feel like the Universe is conspiring against you!

Most of us enjoy sharing stories of inspirational people, and we wonder how they manage. We imagine ourselves given the same circumstances: "I could never be that brave", "I don't have that much energy", "I don't have the resources", "It's too late to start over at this point in my life." We *accept* limitations put on us and therefore we perpetuate our own limited viewpoint.

The obstacles may be real enough – layoffs, health challenges, tragedies, sapped energy, colossal mistakes, loneliness and fear. These things represent the Way Things Are; but, the Way Things Will Be has yet to be determined. How do we move past the limitations of the present moment to the future and the choices it brings? Coaching is about finding the potential in all things.

In my work as a coach and trainer, I have had the opportunity to observe wonderful and exciting transformations as people take charge of their own destinies. I've seen the coaching process work for students in my own coaching school, I've seen it work in the lives of clients working with a coach, and I've seen it work in the lives of the coaches I know.

Coaching involves a strong commitment on the part of the client to be open to new perspectives, and a willingness to act on what they've learned. It depends on a coach who has been properly trained to support the client on their journey without attempting to influence the outcome.

Somewhere along the way, the client becomes clearer, more confident, and more capable of moving toward their desire, no longer hampered by perceived limitations.

Anita has assembled a group of coaches who have had success in using coaching methods with clients of all ages and backgrounds as they move through the triumphs and challenges of their own lives. She has invited these coaches and mentors to share the tools and approaches they use with their clients. It is her intention that this collaborative work will enable you, the reader, to experience a shift in your thinking or perhaps move you to seek out the support of a trained coaching professional.

The coach's role is much like the beacon in a lighthouse – shining its light on the waters, warning of danger, and perhaps spotlighting the options for navigating around the rocks. However, it is the captain of the ship who decides which path he will take. After all, the journey is his to take.

Within the pages of this book, you will find inspirational and practical tips for looking at your own potential in a new way.

Each of us has a limitless amount of light and energy to offer the world. *Life without Limitations* may be the first step to letting your light shine.

Barbara Silva, PCC, BCC
President & Co-Founder
Academy of Coaching Cognition

With Love and Gratitude

This Anthology could never have been conceptualized and birthed without the love and support that I have in my life. First and foremost, I must give Thanks to my Heavenly Father for allowing me this moment to help others believe in themselves once more. I myself have struggled with so many limitations placed on my life from a young age and had decided that no matter what others were like towards me that all people, no matter who they are, have value and greatness within them, including myself!

Love is the key, and having faith in one's self can make a world of difference. Now, where do I begin to categorize the importance of people except by starting from the very beginning?

I would like to take this opportunity to give special thanks to my own personal Mentors, my heroes, my wonderful parents, Jean and Jetty Seergobin, who brought me into this world, and have never given up on me from the time I was a young child living in Georgetown, Guyana, South America. At the age of two, I was extremely sick with gastro and everyone else had lost hope. But my loving parents diligently prayed over me and kept their faith that God had great plans for my life.

My beautiful and loving mom always believed in me and encouraged me when I was sad and feeling helpless in life situations. Mom, you have been like a rock for me through so much. I am honored to say you are my Mother.

My Dad has been the voice of reason in my life. He has always encouraged me to give more to others, no matter what people were like. My dad has always believed in treating everyone with respect and has been a symbol of Integrity and Respect in my life.

My parents have stood by and always believed in me. Thank you Mom and Dad for all that you are, all that you have done, and all that you continue doing in my life and others.

A special thanks to my younger brother, Trevor Seergobin, for encouraging me to follow after my dreams and not to worry about anyone or anything else. You have always been a great source of inspiration and strength for me. I am so grateful to have you as my brother. Thank you for being there when I really needed you.

For the guy who is the love of my life, my husband Stephen Sechesky. Thank you for believing in us and for understanding my relentless pursuit of perfection and being there for others. I'm so grateful and blessed by your love and support, especially patience. Thanks for listening to me and encouraging me to not give up on the impossible, but to help me push myself to the possibilities that are endless. I love you with all my heart. You are truly a blessing in my life and a wonderful daddy for our boys.

I'm so grateful to God for my two darling sons, Nathaniel and Samuel. You put laughter, sunshine and smiles in my days, and help to melt away the stress that life may bring. Thank you for the love, joy and inspiration that you both bring to Mommy every day. I want you each to see how this world that we live in is only shaped by the perceptions and limitations that we carry within our hearts. As we believe more in ourselves, we help others to believe in us. Every human being has a role to change themselves into carriers of love, to cause a domino effect of love worldwide. This is how our future needs to be shaped.

I also want to say a loving thanks to my mum-in-law, Lillian Sechesky, whose life motto is "I can't complain, I have so much to be Thankful for!" You have been an inspiration to more people than you even realize and I am especially grateful to have you in my life. You are such a Blessing to me and so many others in your celebration!

When I had the vision for this book, one of the first people I contacted was my dear friend, Sandi Chomyn. Sandi, you have been the big sister I have always wanted, and I am so blessed to have you in my life. You have always said things straight to the point and never beat around the bush. I appreciate your encouragement for me to step into my 1st Book.

A heartfelt thank you to each of my 29 co-authors. It's been an honor and a pleasure to get to know each one of you. Individually, you have inspired me to appreciate everyone for whom they are and the greatness that is within them. Thank you for your patience in helping me see this "Vision" through for our book! I feel like my family gained 29 more members! All of you guys ROCK!

A warm thank you to Christine Marmoy for believing in me and inviting me to be one of her co-authors in her book anthology "Hot Mama in HIGH Heels", in which I had my debut as an International Published Author with my chapter "Limitations are NOT Sexy!" Christine is now my publisher for this book with her amazing team. Thank you for making my Book Anthology World Class!

There are so many more people to Thank that I can't begin to even name them all. Please forgive me if I missed your name. A few special people stand out not just because of their connection to me, but the impact they have made in my life because of their integrity as leaders, teachers and mentors: Barbara Silva, Mike Klingler and Joanne Dale. Thank you for restoring my faith in myself as a leader that nothing is impossible, no matter how BIG it is. For the rest of you, you know who you are and I love you all just the same. Thank you for your friendship, encouragement, love and support.

If I didn't include the following people from my life who are now departed, it would go against my belief that words have power. My late grandma Seergobin, who named me "Anita" always spoke blessings into my life and told me how pretty I was, how smart I was, and how much she loved me. Every person needs to hear those kinds of words growing up. On her death bed, she told me, "It doesn't matter who doesn't like you, I love you, Jesus loves you, and I believe in you." I will never forget those words.

As well, my late aunt Sherry Ahad, who was also an RN, inspired me to become a nurse. She was a source of strength and inspiration to everyone that knew her. She always told me that I could do whatever I wanted once I had the right education and a heart of love for others.

Finally, my beautiful baby daughter Jasmine Rose, who never had the chance to live her life the way I dreamt it for her. Life is a mystery. We have to make the best of what we have been given in this short time.

In conclusion, I need to address an unusual appreciation to all those in my life who have caused me difficulty, pain or heartache. If it had not been for you, I would not have pursued my healing and the greatness that God placed within me. I forgive.

Introduction

As I reflect over the years of who I am as a wife, mother, daughter, sister, friend, colleague, entrepreneur and student, I have observed how everything that we do in this world comes together like a masterpiece that is created by our personal life experiences. We are the only ones who can control and manage how life will affect us. Our emotional shifts, personal interactions, education, training, health issues, family dynamics, close relationships and childhood dreams are all part of the colorful perspectives of how we paint the picture of our lives. We are the artists that get to choose what we want our picture to portray. My vision for this book was created based on these life experiences. I can truly say it has been a colorful journey so far.

For example, in my profession of being a Registered Nurse for the last ten years, I appreciate having had the privilege of interacting and caring for so many people with various health conditions and challenges. At times I have been saddened by the lives that ended with dreams that were never fully lived. I would think about those lost dreams that were left on the pillows after those people were gone from this world.

Now as an Inspirational Life Coach with 3 levels of training, NLP Practitioner and Law of Attraction Trainer, I have gained so much more insight and depth about how we, as human beings, accept or create our destinies just by the way we shape our attitudes and approach to life. I reflect back over the years and all the lives that I have interacted with and cared for. I have always respected each person as an individual with many facets, and I was not always aware of what they truly presented before me. I have cared for people from all walks of life, from every social bracket, diverse cultural backgrounds and all age groups of both genders. I have treated people of integrity and value, with dreams and ambitions like everyone else who walks this earth.

All individuals, no matter who they are, deserve to be recognized, appreciated and encouraged to have their dreams come true. We are a myriad of people but have the same basic needs for food, shelter and safety. Aside from having our essential needs met, we still desire to feel loved and acknowledged for who we are—someone of Value and Integrity. Imagine how different your life would be today if you were constantly told from the time you can remember that you are important, that your feelings matter and it's OK to make mistakes. Not one of us is without imperfections. This is how we all learn and grow to become our very best!

My book is for those who feel stuck, or for those who feel confident but not ready and not sure why. It is for all age groups, for the young person seeking answers to life's issues, entrepreneurs, professionals, couples, students, and those who need that shift to make a difference in their own lives while they still can. Each one of my co-authors, including myself, is someone just like you. We have been there, walked through similar situations that you may be going through, felt the same kind of fears, tears, frustrations and anxieties of life. We have all had our own challenges and overcame. If we can do it, you can too.

Wherever you are in your life's journey, this book will help you move, shift and transition to the next level. You may be on the verge of making big life-changing decisions—whether it is with your business, career choices, relationships, or just on a personal level to get more satisfaction out of what life has already blessed you with.

Each Chapter has been written with you in mind. Whether you are male or female, this book will speak into your life. You are the focus of this book. Yes, no matter what you are going through at any given time in your life, you will want to have this book close by. It will be a source of strength, empowerment and encouragement to help you. You have 30 mentors at your fingertips to speak into your life with the advice they give on a daily basis to their own clients. You are not alone in this journey.

Now is your time! You can ROCK your own world!

Living *Without* Limitations

Anita Sechesky

A Registered Nurse, Certified Inspirational Life Coach, International Author, Keynote speaker, NLP and LOA Practitioner, Anita studied her Masters in Marketing at the School of Online Business, and is completing her Advanced Life Coach through Coaching Cognition. She is the CEO and Owner of Anita Sechesky – Living Without Limitations. Anita has helped many people from all walks of life break through limiting beliefs in past failures, health, goal setting, self-esteem, leadership, and motivation. She is compiling her 2nd anthology project entitled "Living Without Limitations – 30 Stories to Balance Your Mind, Body & Spirit" to be released in early 2014.

You can contact Anita at the following:

www.anitasechesky.com

Skype: anita.sechesky

✉ **asechesky@hotmail.ca**

f **facebook.com/AnitaSechesky**

f **facebook.com/asechesky**

✗ **twitter.com/nursie4u**

P **pinterest.com/anitasechesky**

in **ca.linkedin.com/pub/anita-sechesky/3b/111/8b9**

CHAPTER 1

DISCOVERING YOUR LIFE WITHOUT LIMITATIONS

Anita Sechesky

When you've come to a place in your life where you feel like you're trapped or struggling, you may begin to feel constraints or chains that are preventing you from spreading your wings to fly. Many of my clients have expressed these kinds of feelings, not understanding why their lives seem like a losing battle of unknown origins. Limitations are things that can start from early childhood and continue building up until they become walls that literally close you off.

In a sense it may feel like you're trapped in a bird cage. You can see everyone else succeeding, achieving and satisfied in life, but with your own limiting beliefs surrounding you, life may feel hopeless. You know you have greatness within you. You believe there is potential for everyone, but you have adapted the mentality or belief that you're not good enough or you're just not meant to live the way you really want to.

As a Life Coach with diverse knowledge and skills, I help my clients by guiding them to express where they feel their limitations are stemming from. I ask them powerful questions and reframe situations to help them change their perspectives. Many of my clients had to face their limitations headfirst to have the courage and determination to achieve a life full of possibilities. My clients discover their own limitations by simply answering my questions or completing assessments.

When my clients express how their dreams look, feel and even "taste," excitement sets in. Once they determine their goals and ambitions, I help them to break them into bite size pieces. When they taste the pleasure of achieving small goals, the prize is closer and realistic now. Goals are dreams that develop inside of us before we even have the skills and abilities to achieve them. My clients work through a series of various exercises building up their confidence, which usually exposes the most profound limiting mindsets. As they tear away the layers of fears, unforgiveness and pain, trapped emotional energy gets released in the form of tears or jubilation. They realize they are free to set new goals once thought of as unreachable dreams. The things that were once weighing them down emotionally and spiritually are now gone.

Through "The Act of Forgiveness," I have mentored many people who have had the most profound breakthroughs. Realistically, we cannot change anyone; we can only change ourselves. Disappointments happen, but they don't need to be the focus of a life seeking joy and fulfillment. Moving forward they realized situations once perceived as negative experiences may not have been as harsh.

You see, when living a life with a limiting mindset, everything around you becomes a misrepresentation of what your life can be. You may feel small or you're in a losing battle with life. Learning to shift your perspectives with a trained coach will help you to feel validated and heal so much quicker than struggling for years on your own. What you carry around inside of you emotionally is what you will attract into your life. You'll only be focused on what you feel.

Here are some key questions about limiting mindsets and perceptions in life:

LIMITATIONS QUESTIONNAIRE

1. Q – Have you ever experienced poor treatment in your life by others?

    A – You may have a baggage of limitations.

2. Q – Do you feel like you're spinning in circles and not going anywhere?

    A – You have no clear direction. More than likely you have a limitation in your life preventing you from succeeding.

3. Q – Do you feel like you're like that bird in the cage?

   A – Your limitations are an invisible cage. Your wings are meant to fly.

4. Q – What kind of environment are you subjecting yourself to?

   A – This could include your exposure to destructive or harsh entertainment (movies, books, and video games), abusive or neglectful relationships, substance abuse, toxic work environments or adverse living conditions.

5. Q – What is your self talk like?

   A – Allowing negative self talk from yourself or others is destructive to self!

6. Q – How do you show up in the world?

   A – Presentation is key to success. Don't limit yourself. Take the extra time that's needed to pull your look together.

7. Q – Do have a hard time forgiving others?

   A – Holding on to resentment and anger will only cause you harm by blockages in your personal perceptions.

My clients have learned that certain lifestyle exposures will directly affect their attitudes, emotions or health. Many people are still afraid of stepping out of their comfort zone, staying trapped by that invisible bird cage.

LIFE WITHOUT LIMITATIONS QUESTIONNAIRE

1. Q – Are you confident enough to achieve success without permission?

   A – Living without limitations does not require consent from others.

2. Q – Do you have a dream?

   A – You have been given a gift from your Creator that's all yours.

3. Q – Can you see your dream happen?

A – When you envision your dreams come to life, you create your realities.

4. Q – Do you have goals hidden inside that direct your steps?

A – Clear, concise and achievable goals equal success.

5. Q – Do you speak positively?

A – Positive self talk and reinforcement increase self-esteem and confidence.

6. Q – Do you step out of your comfort zone?

A – You can't show up in life if you don't step out.

7. Q – How does it feel when you forgive others?

A – Forgiving others releases personal bondages and limiting beliefs about life and people in general. Forgiveness heals!

Many people around us who have achieved success in their lives have learned at some point that they can do it. They didn't wait for permission to be the best that they can be. They didn't let their fear of failure stop them. In fact, it is common knowledge that many people who do succeed have failed many times and learned from their own mistakes, or the mistakes of others.

I allow my clients to express their concerns and help them to understand where their limitations or despair are coming from. We may set goals that are entirely client focused and accountable to me, the coach. With this type of professional relationship, I help my clients explore their own paths in life and what speed they want to move forward.

Clients facing extreme limitations may have a great need for emotional release when trapped by their own or others' limiting beliefs. A number of them have dealt with all kinds of negative life experiences, such as the loss of a loved one, lost finances, job termination, health setbacks, divorce, physical, verbal or mental abuse, and even racial limitations. I have observed how this affects their self-worth and confidence. When they become more focused, they learn how to heal and maintain balance in their lives to be able to be the best for their loved ones.

FOOD FOR THOUGHT!

1. Consider adapting "The Art of Forgiveness" into your life. This is done by setting time aside to reflect on life events that resulted in unpleasant and negative unresolved feelings. This is one of the "Biggest" doors to opening limitations in life. Everything will be affected by those negative feelings—your choices, attitudes, and your health—if you let them fester for too long. They may possibly show up as different forms of stress or anxiety, leading to more serious health conditions.

2. You have to understand and accept that Forgiveness is needed, as you cannot change the past or even other people. You can only change yourself. Decide to recall and write down the names of these people who have hurt you or let you down.

3. When you have listed as many that come to your mind, it doesn't matter how far back you go. Start saying, "I forgive… I now release all of the pain, disappointment and heartache they have caused me."

4. Once you have done this with the entire list, you may find yourself emotionally released quickly. No one should ever have power over you to that extent unless you allow it. Words and things done in the past are in the past. Words have power and negative word cycles can be broken and replaced with positive reinforcement. We cannot change the past but we can choose to make a better future, free of pain.

5. Now that you have done this, it is time for you to recognize how amazing and POWERFUL you really are! You are the only one who can make a difference in your life. Remove your limitations. You get to choose. Choose Love!

If anything that I have shared in this chapter resonates with you, PLEASE contact me. I believe that each one of you has "Greatness" within! Don't let labels, failures, lack, or your own limiting beliefs separate you from the joy, happiness, peace, fulfillment and satisfaction that God and the Universe want to bless you with.

You are valued and greatly appreciated. It's time to spread your wings and fly without limitations. Ready! Set! GO!!

Hanna Hashim

Certified Basic Level Coaching Cognition and Law of Attraction Practitioner, Hanna Elizabeth Hashim mentors others to embrace their birth given right to Unlimited Abundance of perfect health, wealth and happiness. As an English Language teacher in her 15 years career in Britain and Bahrain, she has helped many to improve their language skills enabling them to open up the job opportunities. Hanna was born in Poland, then lived in the UK and now resides in Bahrain with her husband Hashim and two daughters: Zeena and Zarah. Her dream is to set up English Language Centres for the underprivileged Bahrainis and shine the light of hope. She can be contacted on

✉ **beaconoflight2013@gmail.com**

❶ **facebook.com/hanna.hashim.54**

🄻 **linkedin.com/pub/hanna-hashim/1b/878/204**

CHAPTER 2

EMBRACING YOUR BIRTH GIVEN RIGHT TO UNLIMITED ABUNDANCE

Hanna Hashim

Embracing your birth given right to unlimited abundance is a journey of rediscovering your core truths that have been with you since you have come to existence on this earth. Often with time, they got masked and distorted by the beliefs of others and accepted by our subconscious mind as true.

How many people are actually aware that we all were born in the eyes of God as abundant in perfect wealth, health and happiness? Not many I guess. Most of us believe that abundance is something that we need to earn or inherit if we are fortunate enough. Yet the abundance is there waiting for us in equal measures whether you come from the poor or rich background. All we are asked for by the Universe is to believe in it and allow for it to be delivered to us. However, this may not be as easy to accept and understand for many. People, including myself, struggle with embracing this truth, and it takes time, the skills and the intention to fully heal and reprogram our beliefs and reactions to situations so we can live in the continuous flow of unlimited abundance.

Let me take you on a journey to living in this flow. Let's begin by asking ourselves "What do you mean by 'unlimited abundance?' What does that mean to you and what feelings and emotions come to the forefront of your awareness?" From my observations and talks with people this means the following: "having a lot of money, expensive cars, jewelry; feeling happy when we receive a gift or a compliment from others, etc." Society has made us all believe that abundance is about having wealth.

Yet there are other aspects of it that are not mentioned. Living an abundant life is a state of mind where we feel fulfilled in all areas, including abundant health and abundant happiness. So, in fact, it is a mental state of how we perceive things around us. That means that in order to embrace the abundance we need to change our perspective on wealth, health and happiness. We need to heal the emotions of "lack" and shift it into "abundance." Having the attitude of "gratitude" opens the flood doors of unlimited abundance into our lives. Practicing daily "thanks giving to God" creates the vortex for miracles. Being grateful to and blessed by the Creator with things we already have is bringing more of what we desire.

The trick is to look around and savor the beauty of life and see how much we already have. Don't look for ways of dressing up the raw beauty around you; look at it and find the magnificence of it that already exists there. Feel the blessings of being able to see, feel and touch it; and express the gratitude to God for bestowing it on you. This shift in the way you perceive the world around you is "living in abundance."

We place blocks in our subconscious to abundance and achievement. We say, "When I have this I would be happy," but the KEY is to be and feel happy in the NOW; to be grateful for what we have NOW. This brings us into alignment with the vibrations of abundance. We have to feel in every cell of our body that OUR DESIRE IS HERE NOW, even if it is not materialized yet, and feel the gratitude for it. If we feel any kind of negative feeling—sadness, guilt or lack—we are blocking ourselves from receiving what is already ours by birth given right. We sabotage our own flow of abundance by negative self-talk and thoughts. What we need to do, is to think of the most exhilarating event in our lives and feel the feelings that we had then to bring us back into the alignment of receiving. Stay in this state for as long as you can and try to bring gratitude into the forefront; where gratitude resides, the fear and negativity cannot exist simultaneously.

Another block to unlimited abundance may be "feeling unworthy" of receiving the perfect wealth, health and happiness. In my personal observations of people I have been dealing with, the common thread is, "I am not worthy, I am not good enough, I cannot do this job." We self-sabotage our abundance by negative self-talk and lack of belief in our greatness and power. These are within us and are waiting to be unleashed and used to their full potential. Many people give up on their dreams, as they believe that they do not have it in them to bring those dreams into reality. As soon as they stumble across any obstacles they stop, they do not realize that the success may be just around the corner.

We need to feel strong and persevere on our journey to abundance. We will be tested to see how strong our desire is; we need to remind ourselves that the reward is well worth it. You may ask: "How I can do that"; the power of positive affirmations and practicing self-love are the powerful tools that are already available to us. Setting the intention of achievement of our goal allows for miracles to unfold in front of our eyes: the right people come on our paths, we learn the skills we need and the circumstances around us change the IMPOSSIBLE to I'M POSSIBLE. Changing the way we talk to ourselves creates the change of vibrations in our body and surroundings and with that we attract what we actually truly desire. By saying, "I am worthy of a great job, partner, a pay rise etc." you send the message to the Universe that you are ready to receive it. You are embracing your birth given right to abundance.

To fully heal our wounds of lack, we need to embrace the knowledge that abundance does not come from people; the only source of abundance is the Higher Power. Society has made us believe that prosperity comes via a good career, family and the only way to be rich is by either being born into a rich family or work hard. We idolize other people when they give us money or bring us happiness or good health. However, when things do not go as planned we tend to blame others for the lack and mistakes. What we need to learn is that people are only the means of the Creator's generosity to us. We need to remember that His supply is unlimited and we are all worthy of receiving an unlimited supply of money, health and happiness.

In my career, I have worked with people who feel that the society is to be blamed for their lack and unhappiness. What they have not recognized is that the power to change the circumstance lies in the way they perceive wealth. Their social status may not allow them to have access to everything they might want at this moment in time, but faith and change of perspective on who supplies the abundance may bring forth the miracles.

Eliminating the worry, the fear of lack with a Prayer is essential; just say in your prayers, "Dear God, How can I afford this?" rather than saying, "I cannot afford it." This small change in wording opens up the solutions to come forth from unexpected places and people, as God is an Unlimited Supply. He asks us to believe Him, and in the times of hardship we need to stay in faith even more.

Having a passion filled career that brings the abundance of wealth, joy, happiness effortlessly and endlessly is a gift from the Universe. We should look for that gift within us and turn it into a life purpose that brings the fulfillment and nurtures our soul; it serves The Creator and other people in achieving their goals. Many may ask: how to achieve that? My answer would be: spend some time alone and do a little inventory of your life. Ask yourself what is it that makes me smile and be happy when I do it? What comes naturally, easily and brings the joy to me and others? What is mindful and sustainable at the same time? What do you think is the gift that God has bestowed upon you to share with others? These questions might bring up a lot of feelings and uneasiness, as what He wants us to do might not fit in with what we thought might bring the money or what others had in mind for our future. Yet once we follow our "true calling," a massive shift happens. Our job becomes pleasure that brings in the income that is Divinely guided, and this equals happiness and wealth.

Let's open our hearts to the Universe's unconditional love, move from the darkness of our ego-minds into the light of our hearts and souls where He resides. Let's uncover one by one the Core Truths that are hidden there and bring them forward and believe that Unlimited Abundance is our birth given right.

Living *Without* Limitations

Sandi Chomyn

Sandi Chomyn is a life coach known as a Life Management Coach. After raising her three boys, she received her coaching training with Coaching Cognition. She's a farm mom and grandma, inside and out. She has come to enjoy the different facets of her life, by integrating her life coaching business and her love for scenic photography with a healthier lifestyle and good country living. She resides with her husband Bill on a farm in a small farming community in Togo, Saskatchewan, Canada.

www.sandichomyn.com

facebook.com/meetsandichomyn

facebook.com/sandichomyn

twitter.com/sandi_chomyn

pinterest.com/sandichomyn

linkedin.com/SandiChomyn

CHAPTER 3

IN SEARCH OF TRUE HAPPINESS

Sandi Chomyn

To have a happy life you must take on the responsibility of making it happen. There are many emotional barriers that can get in your way to true happiness. By shifting your emotional perception you can overcome all the barriers. You are the only one in the way of what you want that will make you happy, and you do not want to be in your own way! Everything worth having in life, including happiness, takes work. Work, you say? Yes! Happiness is earned. It is created by you and only you. No one can do it for you. You will have to make the changes to make it happen. You will have to start taking action to create the happiness you desire. In order to create that happy life you want, you need to step out of your comfort zone and take action for yourself.

You should think about what you really want in your life. It can be anything from a new home, a change of job, a new relationship, new clothes, joining the gym or a stress free life. You just need to remember it is what you truly want—not what you think you should have or do. What others think should not influence you. So please give this very serious thought. We can see what being happy can mean to a lot of you. It is all those little things in your life that make you happy—like a genuine smile from a child, the sight of beautiful flowers, finding that new love, or laughing with family and friends. Maybe it is making new friendships, building that new home, spending time with your family or just being successful.

It can feel like you are finally enjoying your life to the fullest. Yes, it can simply be that chocolate cake you desire. These are just a few things. I'm sure you can come up with other things on your own.

My question to you is now, "Are you really happy?" Another way of asking can be, "Are you satisfied with your life?" If you say, "Yes," then, that is awesome!! If you say, "No," then you need to think of what will really make you very happy.

By becoming very aware of what really brings you true happiness, you will find that energy and passion in your life that makes you happy. This is something only you can answer. You should be thinking of that one thing that gets you so excited you want to shout it out to the top of world.

Everything will all come clearer and clearer and fall into place, as you start thinking and brainstorming on paper and talking with your coach. For those that are not sure of what I mean, brainstorming is one of the visual exercises I use regularly with my clients.

Being a coach, after talking with you for a while, I would be telling you to get out a pen and paper and start writing. Be specific about what exactly true happiness means to you. What does it taste like, feel like, smell like and look like? How will you find it? What does it mean to you? When do you want it? Why is it important to you? Where do you want to be? Do not worry about what you may think of as being silly or dumb to you—they are not at all that. Let your imagination run wild. Remember it is your true happiness you are talking about and wanting to have. Just let the ideas and solutions flow. The more detailed you are, the easier it will be to take your next step. When you allow yourself to be completely honest, you will discover what needs to change. Do not be critical or judge any of your ideas by thinking they will not work for you. It may just surprise you.

Now that we have identified what brainstorming is, here are a few examples of different things that people are stuck on. I will start you off with questions you can ask yourself. By writing down your answers—maybe to these questions or ones of your own—you will possibly see more things you can ask yourself. Answer those too. Remember these are only examples. Start your own. The next time you go, take them with you when you see or call your life coach and talk about them. You will see that as the questions and answers come, a picture of what you want your goal(s) to be will emerge.

Here are a few examples of how a brainstorming session with a client may go.

My client wants to talk about her health. To my client it can be anything from an illness to overcome to just wanting to lose weight. No matter what, the issue is important to my client. I would start out by asking, "What is your main concern about your health?" An answer can be that my client wants to lose weight. If this is the case this will lead into the question, "What can you do to lose this weight?" My client may reply by saying she could start exercising more and change her bad eating habits. My next question from what my client tells me is, "Is this something you can change on your own, and if so how?" From here my client can go into different ways that she can start exercising more and how she can change her eating habits. As the ideas and solutions flow and I ask my client how this will work for her, she will find the answers on her own that will help her reach her goal of being happy, and find that she is going in the right direction that works for her.

Another common one is a job move. Since this is something that can be well planned or a sudden decision, I would start out by listening to what my client has to say about what brought it on. From what my client tells me this can bring me to asking, "How will it affect you?" He could say that the move did not affect him as much as it would affect his family. This would bring me to the following question, "How will it affect your family?" Here my client will explain his personal situation on why he has to make the move and the effects it will have on his family. A question from me can be, "What can you do to make the move easier?" Here he will answer in ways that may bring on more questions that will bring my client to the answers he is looking for that make everyone happy with the move.

Our finances are another part of our everyday living that can suddenly change. Here is how a brainstorming can go. Client is saying they are having financial issues. This can lead to me asking the following, "How can you go about changing this situation?" The answer may be that she is not sure how to go about it. This can bring me to the question for them, "Who can you get to help sort things out?" By talking more about it, this can have her listing the people that can help them move in the right direction. From here they are starting to see a direction they can go that they would not have seen if we did not brainstorm.

You can see from these three examples how brainstorming works with you and not against you. By me asking my client the right questions from things they have been telling me, this has them coming up with their own solutions that will work for them. Now they can see themselves on the right path on their way to being a happier person and having a happier life.

From this you can see how brainstorming is very powerful. You also noticed from the above examples there are questions that you will have and will want answers for. You could do this on your own. I wouldn't, and can assume you would not either. I tell my clients having a life coach is so much easier and powerful, because it gives you the opportunity to talk about the most pressing issue(s) you are facing right now, and what you feel you need help with. You, with your life coach, will start discussing these ideas, thoughts, situations, and what inspires you to be truly happy. By asking the right questions, your coach will often have you finding you are coming up with a lot of great ideas that you may not have thought of on your own, and some ideas that reaffirm thoughts that you have already had. You never know what new thoughts will come your way. Discover what is getting in the way of having the happy life you want. As you find the solutions that work, you will find your true happiness.

Living *Without* Limitations

Kristy-Lea Tritz

Kristy-Lea Tritz is an inspirational coach and freelance writer. Her work has appeared in *Brio* magazine and local publications. She currently works with couples and individuals, coaching them on how to become connected in an unconnected world, teaching them how to put the puzzle pieces of their lives together. Kristy-Lea also has a passion for special needs children and is currently working on developing products for children and their parents who are affected by ADHD. When she is not exercising her creative side, she is most likely spending active time with her husband Sebastien and son Jacob. She resides in St. Albert, Alberta, Canada.

You can connect with Kristy-Lea at

www.kristyleatritz.com

✉ **contact@kristyleatritz.com**

f **facebook.com/getconnectedcoaching**

f **facebook.com/kristyleatritzwrites#**

🐦 **twitter.com/kristyleatritz**

in **ca.linkedin.com/in/kristyleatritz/**

CHAPTER 4

IN PURSUIT OF PASSION!
INDIVIDUAL, RELATIONAL AND INTIMATE
Kristy-Lea Tritz

Don't be alarmed if this chapter changes your life!

It may change it a little or a lot, but change will occur.

Let me ask...

Have you ever felt that you're not truly heard?

Do you wish your relationship were filled with passion?

Have words like discouraged or exhausted entered your thought vocabulary? Sometimes do you wish you could just give up?

You're not alone. I've coached many couples into knowing there's a better side of life, one of utter happiness. It's all about the pursuit of passion!

Every couple will have struggles throughout their married life. Having the right tools in your marriage toolbox will mean marriage survival. Couples express to me often how they feel they are not heard by their spouse; how a lack of true intimacy plagues them; how the lack of passion and excitement in their marriage is drawing them apart, creating a deep sense of loneliness.

Issues in marriage—or any relationship—don't just happen. They are built one brick at a time. Each person in the relationship helps build that wall of separation.

Couples often try to communicate their wants, desires and dreams to the other, but for some reason it doesn't make its way through into action. Why is this? Is it lack of communication? Communicating effectively is a part of the equation. However, there's an even bigger piece of the puzzle. All the communication tools in the world can't make a person feel fulfilled.

Being in pursuit of passion is like a breath of fresh air. Let's take you from whatever place you are in now, to experiencing what a life in pursuit of passion can be like. Begin to explore living a life without limitations!

PURSUING A PERSONAL PASSION

Why is pursuing your personal passion the most important part of the equation? Everything begins with the transformed you!

As a married person, you can lose who you are. You become a spouse, parent, worker, and caregiver. Today life's roles overtake you, you become lost within these roles. As time goes on, you can feel like you have no identity apart from the daily roles you play. The role is not who you are—it's only something you are capable of doing.

When you become engulfed in who your roles have said you are, your life becomes, well, lifeless! As this process continues, you can begin to feel lonely, isolated, withdrawn and often times discouraged.

So how do you begin to pursue a life of passion if you have an overabundance of roles? Begin by reminiscing of times you've enjoyed in your life most. Is it when you paint, dance, read, travel, mow the lawn? Whatever makes you feel alive! It could even be things you've never tried before, things you dream about, wonder about or yearn for. When you're able to connect with what brings life to the very core of your being, write those passions down. Writing them down brings them into the concrete world, acknowledges them as part of you and allows you to see what lies within the core of your being.

As you begin to explore this area of yourself, you might find a yearning to pursue some of those passions on your list. It is at this point you have begun to enter into the passionate side of yourself. If you will remember at the beginning, I said everything begins as a transformed you?

It is important to make time to nurture within you that passionate side of yourself. It's not about being selfish—it's about being healthy! God created you beautiful with many different facets, and He wants you to allow each one to glitter! You become the most important part of the equation, because truly you are the only one who can change yourself; no one else can do it for you! Roles won't fulfill you no matter how many you take on.

Be willing to reach out, look within and discover who you truly are. Discovering this is a part of the process of living your life with no limitations and having a life of passion! Go for the gold! You're worth it!

PURSUIT OF RELATIONAL PASSION

Now that we started to uncover why it's important to pursue a personal passion, you will see how this transfers into your relational passion with your spouse. This is the next building block of a healthy, fulfilled relationship.

When two whole and passionate individuals get together, they become one unit. If part of that unit is malfunctioning, it will create a ripple effect throughout the marriage. We begin to complain and withdraw. Each spouse, living a separate life, tears at the desire for connectedness, creating an environment of turmoil.

Many marriages live in this state to some degree. It's not about where you are, though, it's about where you want to be, and what you're willing to do to get there. Pursuing relational passion takes a commitment beyond words. It is a commitment of action! Words are just filled with empty air if they're not accompanied by action. Action comes in stages. It takes step-by-step stages that create overall growth. A change is a gauge, measured by steps, some large and some small.

The most important aspect is the answer to this question: are the steps of action bringing me to a more whole healthy life? If the answer is no, then reevaluation may need to occur. If the answer is yes, then ask yourself, "What is the next step? Where do I go from here to continue in the desired direction?"

The most difficult journey is when one spouse is on that journey of change and the other is "stuck in the muck" of their ways. Don't lose heart. Your positive changes can bring great transformation within others. Influence is an extremely powerful tool. Don't lose hope and especially don't lose sight of that passion inside of you.

Marriage partners must be pillars of hope and healing to one another. When couples enter into a partnership of marriage and haven't been in pursuit of passion in their own lives, it can create an environment of toxicity.

Encourage your spouse to nurture who they truly are. It's not about being right — it's about being an inspiration! Encourage each other in the discovery process. Share with each other and keep going forward no matter what!

PURSUING INTIMATE PASSION

Pursuing intimacy has nothing to do with sex! That's right—I said nothing!

Passionate intimacy begins new each day. It begins at the first word or first interaction a married couple experiences during their day. This first interaction will either set the tone for allowing you to be in pursuit of passion or create a drawing away from relationship.

I say sex has nothing to do with intimacy because sex is actually a product of that pursuit of passion daily in your marriage relationship. Learning how to listen rather than hear someone becomes of utmost importance at this step. Without the ability to truly listen to your spouse, nonverbal cues could be missed or simply misunderstood.

What we say is often not what our spouse will hear. Many of my clients have found that learning how to truly listen enhances every experience in marriage. In the beginning, I get my clients to use a guide sheet created as a learning tool for enhancing their communicative process. Once a good habit of listening is established, the rest of the journey to intimate passion becomes far less difficult.

There is nothing more beautiful than a spouse feeling like you've listened to every word they've said. Just like anything else, it's a journey of discovery. Being in pursuit of intimate passion truly means listening beyond words; loving past what you might think are limitations; seizing every moment to build up rather than tear down, and transforming everyday occurrences into experiences. It's then about connecting through these experiences and growing together in a truly intimate passion-filled relationship.

Trust me, when couples get to the point of feeling and knowing those little stepping stone intimate moments to capitalize on, they start to feel fuller within. This creates even more connectedness, and yes, sex will even be more fulfilling and pleasurable because two mutually intimate people will connect on the deepest level. Fill that love tank just like you fill your gas tank and watch your intimate passion-filled life explode!

Every journey, even one in pursuit of passion, will have mountains and valleys. As you climb the mountains of internal dialogue and external struggle, remember that every great change brought to our lives also brings us great learning experience. Failure is not an option unless you allow it to become one for you. Take time to mentor growth within yourself; eventually it will show externally.

Each journey has a beginning and an end. It's what happens within the middle that truly matters. So go forth and live, live your life to the fullest as you embark on your own journey in pursuit of passion!

Holly Osler Bartsch

Holly Osler Bartsch is the Founder and President of Destiny Reigns International. She is an International Author, Mentor, Trainer/Facilitator, Speaker, Visionary Consultant/Counselor and Entrepreneur. Holly earned her Degree of Religious Studies and holds a Minor in Counseling towards her Master's Degree. She loves mentoring people into fulfilling their goals and destiny. For 28 years she has taught and facilitated to all age groups. Holly is happily married and lives near Calgary, Alberta, Canada.

Phone: 1(403)618-8895

Calgary, Alberta, Canada

www.destinyreignsintl.com

Skype: DestinyMentor

Phone: 1(403)618-8895

- hollyvictoriajoy@gmail.com
- destinyreignsintl@gmail.com
- facebook.com/holly.osler
- twitter.com/DestinyMentor4U
- pinterest.com/destinymentor/
- ca.linkedin.com/pub/holly-osler-bartsch

CHAPTER 5

ANSWERING DESTINY'S CALL

Holly Osler Bartsch

You are a champion, waiting to be released. A strong powerful spirit, dwelling in an earthly shell. That's right! You! Magnificent! Transcendent! Eternal-loving! All of you awaits THE CALL OF DESTINY. Sometimes it is a dream, alluring you to possibilities. Other days it is a whisper or prompting that beckons your attention. A "flash picture" of your future in your mind's eye. A longing and desire that has been birthed within. Because you have been uniquely designed and fashioned for "such time as this;" your DESTINY AWAITS. Let's journey together for a moment in time, that will be "kairos" —simply Divine! Come with me...into DESTINY...

Whether you have been on your road of destiny, pursuing your dreams...or plateaued at your "meadow," in peace or internal conflict...or "sick and tired" of facing "road-blocks" and given up on your dreams...or living your life with no strong direction...THIS IS YOUR TIME! Have you ever "mastered" a game, wearing out not only your interest level, but also your need for challenge? It may be a set of goals you have successfully accomplished, leaving you confident and content inside. Or you have plateaued in your life, claiming a time of "rest" or "dreamlessness," desiring to stay within your comfort zone, not wanting or seeing the need to step into the "unknown" yet once again. Have your dreams and goals been put on the shelf for "another time?"

For other people, this is the moment when you can face, head on, your dreaded fears and empty excuses that have kept you "safe," yet bound for years. This is your time for change! You are tired of remaining "stuck," sick of the lies and beliefs that are negative and limiting you. Still yet, you may be one of millions who has yearned to know your life purpose, with no clear specific direction to move forward in.

ARE YOU ANSWERING DESTINY'S CALL? Some of you may not remember much of your childhood or adolescence. Maybe you are not in touch with your heart or emotions to even allow yourself to connect with your inner call. Or you may feel so battered and bruised from certain events in your life that your dreams are stifled, hidden or seemingly dead. Wherever you are at right now, be encouraged to listen closely to the promptings in your spirit. Give yourself permission! You will be amazed at the longings that are still there, waiting for you to step into more of your life purpose. Tune in and clearly identify the truth. Have you forgotten or pushed aside what you already know you are to do? What is your spirit saying to you right now?

IDENTIFY your PASSIONS and DESIRES. Think back to when you were a little girl or boy, through adolescence, leading into your teenage years, into adulthood. Right to this day. Tune in to your heart. What did you lie awake dreaming about at each stage of your life? Write down some of your interests at those times. Remember what got you excited and righteously angry. Both can give you a crisp picture of your innate gifts and abilities.

Most of all, what awakens your spirit? Beauty? Compassion? Pursuing the creative arts? Creating music? Building inventions? Working with children? Medicine? Technology? Public speaking? Solving problems? Eliminating pain, crime, debt, injustice or poverty? Now jot down some of your volunteer and paid job experiences that you absolutely loved. Include the details of when you felt alive and satisfied. Finish up by identifying and recording the common themes in your dreams, desires, abilities and experiences throughout your whole life. What are they?

Are they things like helping others, making people feel good about themselves, encouraging, comforting, mentoring, befriending, etc.? You may be destined to serve others with a heart of compassion and mercy. If you get angry at injustice, you may feel "led" to help others who have been unfairly treated. Remember, YOUR CALLING may be a combination of several skills, giving you opportunity and experience in many fields and spheres of influence. Don't limit yourself. Focus on what you would be doing right now to make this world a better place, if money was not an issue. Walk forward into what you were born to do—make a difference! What will you do today, with your creative abilities, to make that difference in someone's life?

It is imperative and vital that you take the time to delve into your beautiful self. Explore who you are and what you are all about. There is a world waiting for your amazing contribution, as well as your Creator, who made you to glisten! Treasures of your brilliant design will be expressed as you ask family and friends as well. Take courage. Embark on the delightful discovery of you! There is only one of you— YOUR DESTINY AWAITS!

The truth of who you are shines brilliantly when you open your heart and let all the sunshine in. You are loved by others and called to love yourself. Now is the time to connect with all that you have been, and are today. Your identity as a person comes from your character, and knowing who you are, not what you do or the role you play in life. So believe you are good, loving and powerful, making a great impact on many lives. You are a world changer for good! You are surrounded by cheerleaders and friends, past, present, and future, helping you stand strong and tall.

Take time to NURTURE the "garden of your heart." Heal from traumatic, confusing and painful events. Be patient with yourself and others, trusting that you will soon choose to let go of all the "weeds" in your garden. Resentment, unforgiveness, control, gossip, complaining, ungratefulness and negativity are some of the "rocks," "weeds" and "foxes" that could destroy your life and reputation. Clear out all negativity and lies, forever! Focus intently on positive loving truth. Soon you will begin to see new light, experience new joy, and feel more love flowing in and through you! Every choice you make to love others will release you from more blockages and confusion. The greatest mission in life is to LOVE, for it holds the greatest reward.

Your life purpose may seem impossible, because you were created for community and team, and you truly will only be able to fulfill your dreams with their help. Remember, your life mission is not just about you—it is about others! As you move forward by involving others in fulfilling your destiny, they will advance in theirs!

Remember that setbacks help you strategically overcome obstacles. They will make you stronger. Resist defeat and carry on, valiant one! You already have what it takes within and around you!

Make that difference right where you are! YOU ALREADY ARE WALKING IN YOUR DESTINY each day as you make wise choices. Bloom where you are planted! You will find yourself content in heart. You will not wish to be someone else, or covet what they have or are experiencing. Count your blessings each day! Take the risk of stepping into your dream one step at a time and believe. Create an atmosphere for things to happen, and they will! Hold on to faith as you just do it! As you take responsibility for your own life while anticipating open doors to walk through, "divine suddenlies" begin to happen!

One man I have journeyed with shared one particular day how he decided to be happy with his life. He had several months of whining and complaining under his belt, due to years of injustice and pain. Yet a shift in attitude made all the difference! He hoped that his present living space and job would be more conducive to his life goals, so he chose gratefulness, and his whole world changed! He began to announce "sudden open doors" in living arrangements, favor with his Landlord, Employer and friends, received a raise and a new opportunity for community service. He was ecstatic! He chose to let truth prevail to change his circumstances instead of taking revenge, taking control of others or remaining in negativity. He decided to live his best now! So if you are feeling trapped in a "dead end job" or overwhelmed with house, family and present responsibilities, remain faithful with what you have been given to steward. "Promotion" to your next challenge will soon come, drawing you even closer to reaching your goal. WALK OUT YOUR DESTINY DAILY. This is your resolve!

Your inner being craves for the fresh fragrant breezes of new hope to overtake you, whisking you away into fearless soaring to the unknown. Into a realm of endless beauty and color; while conquering giants, saving the world in a meaningful cause, leaving a legacy for others to follow, and gaining a reward for your labor. You are DESTINED for greatness. DESTINY is right here in front of you. ANSWER ITS CALL TODAY!

W. A. Read Knox

W. A. Read Knox is a Certified Life Coach living in Hunt Valley, Maryland, USA.

Read is a Realtor and has experience in numerous businesses over the years involving Aviation, Trucking, Mortgage Banking, Natural Health, Professional Sports, Frozen Foods, and was a licensed Life and Health Insurance and Investment Broker. Read is an avid athlete with a passion for Squash, Tennis, Skiing, Motorcycling, Polo, Hockey, Sailing and Travel. He is fascinated with ReDox Science and its ability to change our health through Bio supplementation.

www.awesomecells.teamasea.com

✉ **Readknox@gmail.com**

f **facebook.com/read.knox**

CHAPTER 6

BREAK THE BLOCKS TO BUSINESS SUCCESS!

W. A. Read Knox

Every businessman or woman knows there are blocks in business. Everybody has blocks at some point in their lives, but not everyone has learned how to benefit from the blocks they encounter. Sometimes when arranged in the right way, the blocks produce competence, integrity, abundance, joy, happiness, trust and confidence. Often wealth is the result of the blocks being built on a solid foundation. Frequently the opposite is true, when the blocks that prevent us from moving forward are due to fear. A coach can help.

Blocks can be used to build or can be torn down to make way for something new. Indeed, there are times that blocks need to be bought or sold, and it is difficult to decide who, what, when, why, where and how to decide. Fear can come up out of nowhere at any time. Have you confronted fear? Has fear prevented you from making choices that were in your best interest?

Why is it that I am choosing to do one thing a specific way, when another way might accomplish more? Fear-based decisions are made every day, and choices that have to be made can often be influenced by fear. Indeed, decisions that should be made are sometimes not made in time or at all due to fear. As a coach, this is where value can be quantified. If instead of fear, a problem or decision is based on love, how will this affect the outcome for the business? How will this affect the business owner? How will this affect the employees? How will this affect the customers? How will this affect the community in which the business is located? How will this affect the local economy? And the ripples venture forth into the universe from the decisions made by governments, business managers and employees and owners, suppliers, and customers. Love-based decisions conquer fear.

"I am a big picture kind of guy," and I can see the value that another set of ears, another set of eyes, and another perspective can bring to a decision that is not being made because of fear. The painful lessons learned by others can be avoided when shared at the right time. Many business owners cannot rely on managers who work for them to help make decisions that should only be made by the business owner. It truly is "Lonely at the Top," as the ears and eyes of the business within the company sometimes must remain "In the Dark" about some decisions that can only be decided by the owner. What is the right decision for the owner is not always the right decision for the employees. A coach who has experience in a variety of businesses and has been through the good times as well as the bad times and even better, the horrific times, can bring a new perspective and new eyes and ears to probe the solutions and strategies to help solve the problems that have the business owner paralyzed in fear. There is nothing quite like working through the tremendous fear caused by a business crisis, and each decision has many potential outcomes.

For example, imagine you have spent millions of dollars building a very successful business with a partner to whom you have given tremendous control over the business. Suddenly you are given an ultimatum to increase that person's salary to twice what they were being paid or they are walking out the door with the majority of the management team to start a competing business. You must decide by the end of the weekend what you will do. Would you be paralyzed by fear?

Imagine you started a trucking company and bought a fleet of tractor trailers and leased them to a company that goes bankrupt several months later. Do you think that there would be a little drama involved in recovering the equipment? What will you do? Would you be paralyzed by fear?

Imagine owning a fleet of new flight training aircraft that are being flown all day every day at a flight school to make the payments to the bank. Students and instructors are extremely busy, and an event of significance happens that shuts down all controlled airspace for months, preventing these students, instructors, and planes from flying. What will you do? Would you be paralyzed by fear?

Imagine building a new hockey arena for $100 million dollars, not knowing if it would return a struggling professional hockey franchise to profitability? Do you think that would be a wise risk to take? What if you had Cancer and might not even live long enough to see your team play in the new building?

Imagine having incredible success and surviving that too!! Are you afraid of success? If so, why? How do you work through this issue if it is present in your life and preventing you from enjoying the fruits of your labor? A coach can help you to figure out what may be in your subconscious mind that may be hindering your success.

Some people have so much success and make so much money that they implode from selfish gluttony, poor diets, alcoholism, drug abuse, "workaholism", or even a sedentary lifestyle. Suicide and depression are very common with exceptionally successful executives and business owners. Often these people are living dual lives that only they know about. They eventually struggle with keeping their secrets; and with the invention of social media, the news travels very fast when it breaks. Some of those who are so fortunate, (athletes and performers in particular) are targets for unscrupulous Bankers, Investment Bankers, Trust Officers, Insurance Salesmen, Attorneys, Accountants, and the list goes on and on. A person who does not know what they do not know can be easily taken advantage of by sophisticated swindlers. As a coach it is important to ask questions that will empower the client to come to the realization of what is best for the client and why. The understanding of the why is the most important part, because this provides the motivation for the client to move through the fear that may prevent them from making appropriate decisions in the first place.

As a coach it is my obligation to empower, teach, share, show, and inspire, support and give the courage to grow. I am honored to help those in need and will do my best to help them succeed.

Healthy affirmations are important for you and the following is one I created for you ...*Now you can Break the Blocks to your Business Success!*

Say it with me... Loud and PROUD...

I am the source of all health.

I am the source of all wealth.

I am a source of inspiration to all who meet me every day.

I am sharing value and knowledge that the world needs and desires.

I am wanted and appreciated wherever I go, and I make a difference.

I am beautiful, and kind, and loving, and supportive, and I care about others.

I exude joy, prosperity, wisdom, love, power and appreciation.

I am grateful for everything and everyone in my life.

I am grateful for pure water, earth, and seeds that create new life.

I am grateful for energy and sunlight, the darkness and the coolness of the night.

I am learning how to be better every day, one day at a time.

I am patient; I know that this too shall pass with time.

I strive for excellence in all that I do so that I may accomplish unlimited success.

What I share with others rewards me greatly in my heart.

I make new friends every day and am open to learn new things every day.

I am motivated by my own heart to bring light to the world.

I strive to know nature as it is shown to me, and I am fascinated with the infinite diversity of its expression on earth and beyond.

I realize there is much that I do not know, but I am eager to be shown how.

I am filled with compassion and want to heal the sick.

I enjoy and am fascinated by all of the creatures that inhabit the Earth.

I am creating heaven on earth. I am blessing and am blessed by all creation.

I am replacing fear with love to enhance my life.

I share my blessings.

So be it, thank you God.

Gwendolyn Weir Swint

Gwendolyn is a Certified Life Coach to the Baby Boomer and Retirement Community, with a niche in Celebrity Coaching in the area of preparation for the "Golden Years."

Gwendolyn is currently co-authoring two inspirational books with two International Best Selling authors.

Gwen and granddaughter, Heather, enjoy living in Detroit's Historic Riverfront community. Gwen has one daughter, Julie and a granddaughter, Helena residing in Hawaii.

Contact Gwendolyn at:

www.gwenswint.com

 GwendolynSwint@gmail.com

CHAPTER 7

WHAT IN THE WORLD ARE YOU DOING AFTER RETIREMENT?

Gwendolyn Weir Swint

As a Life Coach and fellow Baby Boomer with 25 years of service in the senior and retirement community, it gives me great pleasure to relate, connect and share what the "Golden Years" are and are not cracked up to be.

The Baby Boomers are here! Boom! It's your time, your second chance, if you will. Baby Boomers are alive, well, and some kicking higher than others. Some have retired and some are counting and courting the months, weeks and days to the much-anticipated retirement. This brings me to an observation that delights the senses when observed. The next time you come in contact with someone you know that is in the countdown stages to retirement, especially if you encounter them at their place of business, notice their movements. On several occasions I have had the pleasure of watching what I'll call poetry in motion and a ballet all wrapped up in one. I tell you it's beautiful to watch, even though I didn't realize what that flow was about until later, I still enjoyed their whole demeanor. It also reminded me of some of the smoothest rhythm and blues moves you can imagine. What an exciting time that must be.

I say what an exciting time that must be, but I failed to mention that some baby boomers have no intentions of retiring anytime soon, if at all. Of course they have their own reasons for which I don't have the space to go into here. I will say some are creative and have no desire to give up their creativity. Some think this is just how life goes and they go right into traditional retirement. Then there is a percentage of retirees looking for something constructive to do after returning from that dream vacation. You see, retirement is not what it's cracked up to be. You don't just come home and live a life of leisure as many still dream of doing. How does that rock your world?

The point is, while we are planning our financial portfolio, social security or pension benefits, should we not include time management? We like to think of our retirement years as the "Golden Years." We treasure this time and look upon it as being more precious than gold, so we want to spend it wisely. Some may say, "Well it's too late for that now." Truthfully speaking, it's never too late. If you woke up this morning able to think for yourself, your time left on this earth is still of value. You can still make worthwhile contributions, which in return contribute, partly, to your own well-being.

Zooming in a little closer I would like to share with you what I have observed during my 25 years of service to this unique community. In the area of time management, it is practically nonexistent on the level of contributing back to society or even within the community. This is not a judgment or a putdown, it is clearly an observation. The reasons I hear are, "Oh, I'm too old, too tired or too sick." "I've worked all my life and I want everything I've got coming to me." Understandably so, but the truth is, life just isn't going to support that. Let's face it, my dearest friends, life will always remain a great game of giving and receiving whether you participate or not. Plain and simple, no giving, no receiving. Truth is we're really always giving and receiving, but are we conscious givers and receivers, and are we giving and receiving with love?

Let's take a short trip down memory lane. Remember how hard you worked to provide for your family? It left you very little time to think about what you might want to give back to the world. You know that idea you have that still surfaces every once in a while. The one that would make life easier for everyone. Now that you're retired or getting ready to retire—and after that dream vacation, of course—tell me. Would this be the perfect time to explore and discover some of those untapped ideas? Tell me, if you can, why do you think you were born, and what do you think your purpose for being here is? These are two of the most important questions you could ask yourself, especially if you're at all interested, or not sure of how to go about living your "Golden Years" on purpose. Don't allow anyone to suggest that it's too late for you. Let that be your decision, and then question yourself if you think it's too late, because under most circumstances it is never too late to do anything that you are inspired or motivated to do.

Supporting and caring for family was but for a season, and you did it! Now it's time for you. I'm not speaking of a life of leisure because we know that's the illusion that sucks you into what I see way too much in the senior community. With all that time on hand, there's plenty of room for the gossip club to form itself. Something like the bar where everybody knows your name, except in this community that includes most of your business, as well. No escaping that, no matter how hard you try. Not that they want it that way. It's just that no one addressed the issue of time management for the Golden Years. You know all too well what happens when you don't have a plan. When you don't have a guide to follow, you leave yourself open to all sorts of things associated with the illusion to enter such as I'm too tired (low energy), I'm too old or I'm too sick (thoughts of senility). Those are not thoughts of well-being.

You can only have a series of thoughts of well-being when you are making positive contributions and interactions with others. Practice eating healthy, exercise, plenty of fresh air and sunshine all contribute to your well-being. Now you can see why it is not healthy to chase that dream of leisure for your Golden Years. I see many baby boomers following that path; you don't have to. Plan your time purposefully. I'm a witness to what happens when you don't. You've survived a lot to get to the Golden Years, they are too precious to waste. Learn how to live them with the least amount of stress as possible.

Since communication with you, for now, is only through these few pages, I would like to give you a sampling of how you can jumpstart your Golden Years.

5 POWERFUL QUESTIONS TO ASK YOURSELF WHILE CONTEMPLATING YOUR GOLDEN YEARS JOURNEY

1. What do you want those years to feel like?
2. Who in the World do you want to spend those years with?

3. Where in the World do you want to spend them?

4. What will you do to maintain your health, well-being and independence for as long as possible?

5. What do you want your Golden Years to look like?

These precious gems (The Golden Years) can be what they're cracked up to be. A little planning is the key ingredient.

Planning on living your Golden Years in a Senior Citizen Community?

3 SIMPLE QUESTIONS TO THINK ABOUT

1. Besides what management is telling me about this lovely community, what else do I need to know?

2. Do I need to visit at night to see what that environment is like?

3. Should I ask current or past residents what the living experience in general is like for them?

Do you see, now, how you can skillfully plan out those glorious years and have the quality of life you didn't think was possible? Can you see that it doesn't matter how much or how little money you have? What matters is the conscious effort you put into the design. Comparing yourself to others and secretly or openly wishing you had their lifestyle. Thinking that you should have what they have, because, of course, having what they have you could do it so much better than the way they're doing it. Right? Please, my dear friends, spare yourselves of the stress and heartache that desiring what others have will bring. There is nothing lacking in this world. When you look at a tree does the tree appear to be lacking any leaves? Does the ocean lack fish? Are there any birds lacking in the air? Are we not greater than that? Have we not been given dominion over every little and big thing on earth? What's your life decision, dearest friends, have you decided to be a have or a have not?

I am so grateful and humbled for this opportunity to chat with all of you. My sincere hope is for The Golden Years to be the best years of your life.

Living *Without* Limitations

Pat Campbell

Pat Campbell is an Online Business Consultative Coach. She has completed training in Coaching Cognition. She currently is apprenticing as a Certified Trainer within a training platform, Daily Marketing Coach.

Pat is author of two eBooks: *The 9 Ultimate Shortcuts to Getting Leads Online* and, *Insider's Secrets to Marketing S.M.A.R.T.*

Over 17 years of network marketing, Pat has learned the necessity of managing her entrepreneurial ventures alongside a full-time commitment as a Registered Nurse and to her family.

She embraces the truth that the power of her mind forges her personal success. She is keen to help others discover that truth.

www.patleecampbell.com

✉ **pat@patleecampbell.com**

f **facebook.com/PatCampbellBiz**

f **facebook.com/pat.campbell.7315**

🐦 **twitter.com/campbellp**

in **linkedin.com/in/patcampbell2**

CHAPTER 8

REFRAME YOUR MARKETING MINDSET
Pat Campbell

Are you positioning yourself as the CEO of your business, accepting all responsibility for both ups and downs of marketing? As a Business Consultant, I coach clients to find their strengths to reframe, refine and own a mindset that empowers success.

When you think of using the power of your mind to move your business forward, think of renowned athletes. The truth is, that like these individuals, you can train your mind to have a fine-tuned, savvy marketing mindset. Whether you are a beginner or veteran, you are empowered to sharpen your business skill sets. You have the power to decide to make changes and implement them. No one can take that power away from you.

Do you know that every successful entrepreneur has worked their way through a process of enjoying business growth, alternating with periods of losses that tempt them to quit? In consulting, I help clients to be aware of those patterns, and equip them to mindfully choose persistence.

So what makes a Marketer's Mindset different?

Entrepreneurs are not satisfied with the limitations of living their lives according to the agenda of their employers; they yearn for more. It is the hunger to truly have freedoms that are based on their values that energize employees to search for ways to create a new lifestyle for themselves.

That is the early mark of an entrepreneur—committing to whatever it takes to build their own income streams. They accept the rigors of self education, setting aside entertainments, disciplining their work schedules, facing business upswings and downswings. A marketing mindset has a huge appetite for savvy business strategies to learn, implement and teach.

The freedom to give generously, to live anywhere, serve as inspired, travel at will, retire early, be debt free, live according to your own agenda. These are freedoms entrepreneurs enjoy that are different from the mindset of those content to work week in and week out, year after year building someone else's dream.

Yes, I used the word "rigors." Earning the freedom privileges of entrepreneurism comes by showing up every day for your business and working hard. Many, like myself, are building their business alongside of paid employment. That's how it is; it demonstrates the commitment to yourself and your goals to sacrifice time from family and friends to get to that place of freedom.

Business owners with enterprising mindsets are networking, reading, learning. If you are hoping for a quick and easy path... rethink what your intentions are.

Using our analogy of athletics, entrepreneurs beat their personal best by pushing to perform past their comfort zone. Athletes hire a coach, they fine tune techniques, and train hard to position themselves in front of the competition.

Marketing is the sport of business. I don't mean that in jovial tones, but am referring to the discipline of athleticism. Like the athlete, make up your mind to make the necessary changes. The mind has the capacity to change, to be trained to perform however you choose to serve you best. You have to find a trusted coach and push yourself hard.

Train Your Marketing Mindset to:

1. Become aware of successful people, watch their work patterns, and get insights to how they think with close attention to their content—business.

2. Learn how entrepreneurs control their thoughts; creating habits that influence their business success.

3. Sharpen your mindset daily in order to be prepared to deal with challenges as they arise. Deliberately set time aside daily to read favorite quotes or short passages from inspiring authors. Don't take your entrepreneurial commitment for granted, you have to cultivate it. Surround yourself with people who have a positive outlook in the entrepreneurial space.

4. Use imagery to reinforce your goals in business. Gathering pictures, words and ideas is more than a visual reminder. They have a physical impact on your brain, committing you to and attracting a successful business.

5. Soak up all the influence and information possible to move towards success. When you are watching your world, observe how commerce is done, how sales are made, whether in retail, TV, or written media…take physical notes so you can capture ideas to repurpose into content. Do not hoard the information to yourself. It's very important to pass it on via Social Media, blog posts, or even sales pages!

As a business owner, be a leader. Leadership accepts the fact that both success and failure rest on your shoulders. Are you ready to take responsibility for that?

Experiencing "failure" along your journey is a sign of growth, demonstrating that you have pushed past a comfort zone to implement a new skill or strategy. This is not the time to quit. It is the time to re-evaluate, consult with your coach, peers; regroup and try again.

Failure is a common experience of entrepreneurs. Success is tracked by an upwards trajectory. Then something happens in business momentum, and there is a downward slide. You pull yourself together, moving upwards only to find yourself down another slippery slope. A few cycles of this and many, many marketers quit, not realizing that the next graph up reaches their goals. Every successful entrepreneur has worked through these valleys. You can train your mind to recognize these growth patterns of success tempered with down times as necessary for success.

In retraining your business brain, you are accepting the consequences of all your decisions. Perhaps you have spent lots of time and money, not receiving the expected return on your investment. This is the time to lay aside all blame. Laying blame on others is a totally unacceptable state of mind. Accept the consequences of each decision you make, find the lesson in your disappointment and move on.

When you are using your business savvy well, you create experiences for your customer resulting in purchases. This is powerful influence. As a marketer, always be mindful of who your ideal customer is. Write your blog post, post in Social Media, create products such as video, eBooks, PPT presentations, courses for your ideal customer. Realize that you have influence over others' behaviors. You have a duty to be mindful and responsible with that influence.

Your marketing mind has the wonderful capacity to see the world differently, take in information and implement action to change the course of your business. It is important for you to develop systems to conduct your business in order to avoid becoming overwhelmed taking in huge amounts of new information. Systematic approaches to your business allow prioritization of business actions.

System examples are:

- Start every day with focus on affirmations, business quotes or other inspiring resources to prepare your daily schedule.
- Make a habit of spending an allotted period of time in Social Media daily.
- Accumulate content ideas to post to Social Media or write blog posts regularly.
- List and follow through on Income Producing Activities.
- Set up your training, and personal/business development time.
- Be accountable to yourself daily by listing at the end of your work day all the activities you have done and forming a list of priorities for the next business day.
- Fit in exercise.
- Schedule your work activities around your family's needs.

- Over time, create a Standard Operating Procedure (SOP). Many successful business owners who sell their businesses, developed SOP to ensure that the new owners continue to have success

- An SOP also keeps a new entrepreneur from being overwhelmed.

By developing a standardized system to conduct business, you are empowering your mind by putting things in order and implementing action. You also give your mind the ability to take in more education to implement into your business.

Overload of information is crippling. If you continue to take in volumes of information without taking any action, your brain feels like it cannot take in anymore and "stalls." Taking action, even if it is not perfect, gives your brain room to step back and evaluate, then make changes required to achieve better results.

Be on the lookout as you are developing your keen marketing mindset for an area of expertise you have. If you strategize how you can position yourself as an expert in a single area of your business, you further develop leadership. No matter what business you are in, there is an opportunity for you to offer unique value to your team and customers.

Think of influential marketers in your circle. Note how they have positioned themselves as experts in at least one area of training. There is something you are good at. Take that knowledge and find a way to package it in a format that appeals to your Ideal Customer.

You can acquire a sharp marketing mind by making a decision to get the training, take action, and seek accountability with marketing steps. You can choose to train your mind to perform. You are not limited in any way to a pre-set pattern of thinking. Let the power of your mind move your business towards your goals.

Viviana Andrew

Viviana Andrew is a certified coach and online business consultant. She was born in Indonesia and currently resides in Malaysia. Her strength is in networking and online marketing. She has built an extensive network through her online business and overcame her limiting belief by embracing an empowering belief, "I believe in success". Her mission is empowering solo entrepreneurs to build an online business with passion, clarity and uniqueness.

www.vivianaandrew.com

f facebook.com/InternetNetworkMarketingSuccess

f facebook.com/VivianaCoaching

○ twitter.com/coach_viviana

○ youtube.com/user/viviwid09

○ pinterest.com/vivianaandrew

○ linkedin.com/in/viviana

CHAPTER 9

INSPIRE YOUR AMBITION

Viviana Andrew

If you have lost your ambition for success, you are not alone. Our hectic life keeps us busy and prevents us from focusing and nurturing our ambition. If you want to achieve big results in life, you need a big ambition, not a small one. What is it like to inspire your ambition? Have you ever dreamed of becoming a successful person or achieving beyond what you are today? When you inspire your ambition, you live with a mission and you start to bring out the best in you. How can you inspire your ambition? First, you need to find your source of inspiration and then empower your inner self.

FINDING YOUR SOURCE OF INSPIRATION

What is inspiration? It is the spark or flame that ignites and starts a fire in you. When you are inspired, you feel a strong passion within you. Your mind and soul will be stimulated and you will be moved to action. You will want to channel all your energy into something that you want so much to do. So finding the source of your inspiration is important in your quest for bigger and better things. What inspires you? Or who inspires you? What it is about the thing or person that gives you that inspiration? Could it be famous quotes that get you motivated? Or the success of the person that makes you want to emulate them?

Knowing what inspires you is important. You will seek similar inspiration, which can refresh and give you the fuel to keep going. You will wake up every morning with excitement for what you want to do for the day, and go to bed with a feeling of satisfaction after accomplishing what you set out to do. Find your source of inspiration. This is the first thing you need to do. Once you have found it, use it and incorporate it to your ambition. Next, move on to challenge yourself.

Challenge Yourself

Get yourself out of your comfort zone. If you have never made any significant improvement in your life, you must not let yourself feel down. Believe you can make a success of yourself. Start by saying, "I believe I can be successful." Do you remember feeling great after achieving something when you were young? Would you want to get the same feeling again? So take action now. Take up a challenge or join a competition, something that you want so much to do and get a sense of achievement upon completing or winning it. Of course, success does not come instantly overnight. But you have already set yourself on the right trajectory. You will also have embedded a belief in yourself in your subconscious mind. You have planted the seed in your thoughts that you can be successful. You now need to ensure you keep that within you by tapping on positive vibes.

Tap the Positive Vibe

Tap on the positive emotion as it drives a positive action. How would you imbue your thoughts with positive vibes? Have you ever felt grateful for the good things that you have today? Have you helped someone and felt the appreciation from the person? Have you made someone's day? Positive feeling is good because it is self-motivating. It raises your emotional intelligence too. The positive energy will give you the momentum to move forward.

EMPOWER YOUR INNER-SELF

A big ambition needs empowerment. When you feel empowered, you will be driven to success. You will set the goals toward achieving your ambition. You will set your bar high as you will want to achieve big things. When you are empowered, you will feel invigorated. You will enjoy what you do today. You will always look forward to tomorrow. You will maximize your potential. How many of you are aware that an average person uses only 10% of their potential? There is still a lot of room to grow or expand and to discover more of your hidden talents and gifts. There are 3 steps to empowering yourself: knowing yourself, finding your ambition and taking actions for your ambition.

KNOWING YOURSELF

Knowing yourself is the power that can help you manage your emotion successfully. If you can manage your emotion, you can manage destructive behaviors like anger, sadness and jealousy. Those feelings will make you regress in life. You will then choose to behave positively.

Knowing yourself also means believing in you. You believe you have the power to make a difference for yourself. You believe you are unique; you have immense talents and strengths to achieve what you want and to succeed in what you do.

You live by what you value in life. If you know what you value, you can then make an important decision like how you want to live your life, and what career and the type of business to choose.

Knowing yourself means improving you.

Finding Your Ambition

Do you really know what your ambition is? Do you keep changing your decision, go with the crowd or be swayed by those who probably do not have your interest in mind? Stop and think for yourself. Think of what you want in life. How will you find your true ambition? It must be a strong desire that comes from your heart. Think of the time when you were young, you wanted to be the person who had the greatest influence on you, and who you would aspire to be when you grow up. Perhaps you want to be the doctor, teacher or fireman. Or think of what you are good at. Where do your talents lie? Would you want to be able to do the kind of work with what you know or have? Like public speaking or speech writing. When you find your ambition, you will feel a sense of purpose. You will then be determined and greatly desire to succeed. It will fire your spirit and you will be able to unleash your ingenuity and creativity. You will be excited by what you are doing and you will not need to be pushed.

Taking Actions for Your Ambition

After knowing what your ambition is, you must start taking actions for it. Ask yourself these questions:

- What is your goal? Is it different from what you are doing currently?
- What do you need to do to accomplish your goal? When is the deadline?
- What difference would it make for you and the people around you when you have achieved your goal?

Know your goal and work towards it. You will encounter obstacles along the way or something may cause you to go off course. Find a means to overcome those obstacles. Get back on course when you discover that you have strayed. Keep your goal within your sights. Focus.

KEEP YOUR AMBITION INSPIRED

Once you are on your way to achieving your ambition, you need boosters to keep the ambition alive. This will be the support from other people and your own affirmation.

Network with Great People

The reason why my ambition does not die off is because I network with great people. I believe in what the law of association says, that the five closest people in your life will determine your future. You need a mastermind group whose members can support each other. How do you feel when people support, encourage and give you feedback? You feel empowered, right? You have to stay close with the group so your ambition does not die off.

Get Support from a Coach or Mentor

Every athlete has a coach to help maximize his performance. Every young executive will have a mentor to assist him. You need a coach or a mentor too. What role does this person play? A coach helps you to find solutions to your problem and develop your potential. A coach brings out the best in you. A mentor can guide you and give you advice when you are out of ideas. A mentor is a person who has been there and done that, who knows what you are going through and can show you the way as you develop.

The Power of Affirmation

Use the power of affirmation. I AM, I BELIEVE, I LOVE are powerful words of affirmation. State your ambition as clearly as possible using active verbs. For example, "I am building my online business successfully." When you say I am and it is followed by a positive statement, you reinforce the feeling of empowerment and renew your faith in your abilities.

You will live a more fulfilling life and grow when you inspire your ambition.

Patrick Hayden

My passion is to help myself and others achieve success. Growing up in a middle class family showed me the necessity to achieve. My Mother often asked me to fix things. She would say, "You are gifted with your hands, you have the patience of a saint." Her passing was my downfall, but her inspiration helped me discover who I am.

Finding my passion, innovating and creating things, to help others, I was awarded a Diploma in Psychotherapy and Hypnotherapy.

I am now enjoying my work as a Life Coach and inventor.

Living in the NOW!!!

Patrick Hayden
41 Ministers Park, Lusk,
Co. Dublin, Ireland.
Mob: 353 + 086 313 07 23

www.thegreatlightconnections.com

✉ patohayden@gmail.com

f facebook.com/patrick.hayden.96

🐦 twitter.com/PatoHaydo

📌 pinterest.com/togethers/pins/

in linkedin.com/home?trk=nav_responsive_tab_home

CHAPTER 10

HOW TO BE ORGANIZED FOR SUCCESS
Patrick Hayden

"Organization dissolves frustration, anger, stress, impatience and many many more, which we will discover on the way."

Patrick Hayden 18/12/2011

Getting organized is one thing; keeping the order is another. Most of us are organized to a certain degree, lots of us are comfortable with a low level of organization, and a big majority of us live a life of clutter—both in our homes and our minds.

Organization is one of the most important ingredients of success. Have you ever gone to a meeting and, when you got there, you found you have mislaid something? Or worse, during the meeting, something is brought up and you never thought of it, but it was so obvious to everyone else that it made you look stupid? Well, this sort of disorder lowers your self-esteem and raises your level of frustration. Everything you have done, all you are doing and everything you will ever do, will be a menu. What is meant by this?

For many years, I have been trying to understand life's ups and downs, how one wins and another loses. As a professional Coach I have worked with many clients who experienced this type of lifestyle, clutter and disorder. We all have experienced the part of the mind that keeps us in oblivion, cluttered and disorganized. How to recognize this part? Have you ever been doing a job and you take something out of the drawer, cupboard, or toolshed and after you have finished the job (catch this), the disorganized part of the mind will at that very moment say to you in a nice, soft voice, "Leave that there, you can put it back later." So you leave the item there. This sort of thing happens many times and before long, you have a room cluttered.

This is a habit, and we tend to exercise it 'till it becomes automatic and instilled in us. How can we abolish this habit? Most may say, "Just tidy up after yourself." This may work for a short time, but old habits die hard. How will we achieve organization every time? When you hear the little voice saying, "Leave that there, you can do it later," recognize that this is the ALARM to tell you to answer that voice, by saying, "NO, I'LL DO IT NOW." There's a lovely quote that came to me, while working with some of my clients, some years ago when a thought comes to mind that something has to be done or dealt with, DO IT NOW; when you act immediately, instant happiness and success is what you achieve, so... "DO IT NOW". Copy this quote and write it down, place it in areas where there is clutter, this will help to remind you each time you need to be organized.

I want you to achieve organization for success, if you make that little change, you will enjoy huge results but if you listen to that little voice saying, "Leave it, you can do it later," failure is guaranteed. This little change is the first step to awareness, the true you (law of abundance).

Frustration is a huge part of modern day life, what is meant here is frustration keeps us in oblivion, a prison hard to escape. Frustration only exists because of disorder, the only thing that beats frustration is organization, nothing else; there is a part of our mind that keeps us busy with everything but organization.

If you are reading this chapter, it's clear you want success NOW! I want you to stop reading, get yourself a notebook, follow this exercise to the letter and success is guaranteed; in fact, it will be impossible for you to fail. Now, how will you succeed? Because this system has been put together to achieve complete order, and you will see how you have failed in the past by going through the steps that you used in the past and checking those steps with this new system. Please do not skip this step, as to do so, you will have given in to the part of the mind that holds 99% of the world's population back. My clients could explain what I mean here, but it would take another book to cover this sentence. I want you to trust what's been said and at least try this system.

Okay, what is the system? Let me say, this system is so simple, this is why it's missed. The system is called "A-Z Menus." What does this mean? Well as was said earlier, everything you have done, all you are doing and everything you will ever do, will be a menu. Take a look at all you have done and see that everything then had ingredients, which in turn were menus.

Take a look at this, get your notebook and open the first page; at the top left hand side, write the word "Menu" and a title of your next mission or task. Let's pick a task, say it is a "garden makeover." If you, like many, don't write anything down then the menu is in your head. So let's try this exercise now; write everything down under the word "Menu" and write each task on separate lines under each other. Now the menu is out of your head and on the page. Think of what should be done first, second, etc. and put the appropriate number in front of each task. Now you will be surprised to see the disorder of the "head-menu;" strangely the last thing in your menu will more often be the first thing that will need to be done and all the other numbers will be mixed up. How will this make any difference? Well by doing the tasks from your "head-menu," you will lose time and money, this has been a proven strategy for generations.

The strange thing is, if you use menus from your head, you will fail. Always remember, money and time used properly = success. How will a menu written down save me time and money? Because you will complete the tasks of that menu in the Right Order. For example, would you walk up a ladder starting at step 9, then 6, then 3? No changes results in no loss of time because time is money.

"But if I do it from my head, I will still get it done;" sometimes yes, but more often no. "How can you be so sure of that?" Okay, it's time to show. This example below shows you how you will fail if you use your "head-menu."

MENU: GARDEN MAKEOVER:

(Head-menu)

Dig garden
Lay patio

COMPILED BY **ANITA SECHESKY**

Plant shrubs
Hire a skip
Garden plan
Build walls
Clear rubbish

So let's carry out these tasks in the order that came from your "head-menu." Dig garden—where is the rubbish going? I have not ordered the skip; that is number 4 in your "head-menu." Moving on, number 2 of the "head-menu" is lay patio—where will I lay the patio of which I have no plan for because that is number 5 in the "head-menu." Moving on, number 3 of the "head-menu," plant shrubs—I have a heap of rubbish in the way and the patio slabs from the builders merchants has arrived. Surely if I plant shrubs they could get broken or damaged. And number 4: hire a skip. So, it is clear to see the disorder of the "head-menu" and how it will cause huge frustration and a loss of time and money. It always amazes me how the sequence of the "head menu" comes out mixed up, every time. These menus become fun and success is sure.

My clients now enjoy the A-Z Menus system, they tell me it has really helped them, and that they haven't felt frustration since they have started using the system.

"Organization is the Mother of success".

Organization eliminates procrastination, failure and frustration; killing these three will lead to a life of success, for sure. What will you achieve if you use the "A-Z Menus System?"

1. Awareness = Happiness

2. Organization = Success

3. Personal Development

4. Motivation

5. Eliminate frustration, forever

Living *Without* Limitations

Stacey Cargnelutti

Stacey injects you with pure passion! She awakens the spirit with eternal truth that heals and frees, and launches souls into destiny. Her energy is contagious! The inspired words that flow from her spirit restore and redeem lives. She helps you rebuild, reframe and reignite the life, liberty and authentic pursuit of happiness within.

Stacey awakens the spirit by stirring up the unfailing love of God woven into the fiber of all mankind. Her work as a writer, teacher, speaker, life, faith and fitness coach, has helped many transition from the stormy seas of life to the calm landing of a sandy beach. It is at the water's edge that her work is showcased.

Contact Stacey at:

www.staceyc.com

- ✉ **stacey@staceyc.com**
- ✉ **Stacey@Stacey43759650**
- f **facebook.com/staceyccom**
- f **facebook.com/stacey.cargnelutti**
- in **linkedin.com/profile/view?id=198977769&trk=nav_ responsive_tab_profile_pic**

CHAPTER 11

UNSHAKABLE YOU

Stacey Cargnelutti

No wobbles, no flab! Are you ready?

Do you know the emotional roller coaster of caring too much about what others think and misplacing your confidence? Time and again you find yourself jumping through hula-hoops in attempts to gain the approval of man and place your trust in the ever-changing realm of the natural, rather than the unseen, eternal nature within.

If so, my guess is that you're ready for some higher ways and better things! Well, get excited, because there are some new places and wide-open spaces waiting to free and fulfill you like never before.

The goal, coming from a seasoned life, faith and fitness coach, is to be strong, firm and lean, in body, soul, and spirit. You are to be established and motivated to go, do and be, all that you are designed and destined for.

How does it sound to 'cut the fat' and remove every obstacle that weighs you down and throws you off course?

Excess weight of any kind serves only to keep you from fabulous YOU!

When you make a decision to discover and align with the true you, it's like putting wings on, the sure evidence that you are ready to soar. More often than not, appearance and performance seem to speak louder than inner strength and fortitude. Therefore, it's common to see many searching for solutions in the ever-changing realm of the natural.

Ultimately, mankind seeks only to find his worth as a person. "Outsourcing," or searching for one's worth through the acceptance of others, is a surefire strategy to defeat.

So the struggle remains in connecting with the strength and beauty lying dormant within, and conquering the wobble that moves you into shaky places, as well as the "spiritual flab" that drives all empty pursuits.

To be unshakable is to be certain, sure, confident, bold and courageous. Most will agree, it's a rare quality these days, and because it is rare, it is very noticeable when it shows up.

True security is evidenced by confidence. It shines bright, and is the key to life's great treasures and deepest pleasures. Oh, and the bliss of true contentment. Whether you're looking to build a body, a relationship, business, future, family, or better life, a calm, courageous confidence is your master key. How many secure people do you know? Ones who take interest in the opinions of others, but are not held captive by them?

When you've answered life's big questions, "Who am I?" and "Why am I here?" unshakable confidence rises up within, doors seem to open, and the world looks on to see, support and celebrate you and your mission.

Yes, you are to be celebrated not tolerated.

Are you celebrating the gift of you?

And the doors, well you'll find that they've been open all along.

WHY DO THE DOORS APPEAR SHUT?

So the girls come to me wanting a new body, more romance, power, energy, clarity ... "I want to lose weight." "I want a better relationship." "I want to get my life together."

These desires are followed by an endless list of self-judgment statements such as, "I'm fat, lazy, undisciplined, uncoordinated, unattractive, unlovable..." and lastly, said in a myriad of ways, "I'm messed up!"

Most have a real good reason why they know they're "messed up" and "unlovable," but they don't always see the correlation between their "knowing," and the life this "knowing" has produced. Could a "faulty knower" be the source of their pain?

At the root of all the "wants," is the primal need for acceptance, love and honor, the Divine kind that requires nothing in return and nothing in advance. No it's not too much to ask for.

The big lie, "I know that if I can just lose weight, do more, get my body back … 'he will want me,' 'I will get the job,' 'others will applaud…' The bottom line, 'I will be alive, worthy of love and happy!'" Nope.

Faulty "knowers" continue to compel vain and futile pursuits of men and women around the globe. The weight, the appearance and the performance are not the problem; therefore, they will never provide the solution or act as the butler that opens any door to self-worth and success in life.

THE CULPRIT

Insecurity is the fruit of an ego-driven life. It lives to confirm its' belief that love is dangerous. When love is dangerous, life is not known. For the source of life is love.

I work with ladies who have never been seen or heard, who know the feeling of "invisible," and believe they exist to satisfy the self-centered needs of others.

And the men, well they speak from places of apprehension, seeming to be out of touch with their God given, authentic strength, and the effortless power that flows from true Divine connection.

Behind the self-sabotaging ways of perfectionism and martyrdom, and the ego-driven space where fear works to blind all from the Divine and powerful nature within, is magnificence, beautifully wrapped in a glorious purpose-driven passion waiting to be unleashed.

What if everything you need was already here? What if the door was already open? What if you became the person you respect others for being, right now? What if you believed that your dream was God's plan for your life? How would things be different?

You are the brilliance of an exquisite and costly diamond, and you carry the determination and courage of a triumphant warrior! But will you believe that? Discovering and connecting to your own values and beliefs is the firm foundation real life is built upon.

Being tossed to and fro by the opinions of others results in disordered eating, body image distortion, selfish ambition, vanity, self-sabotage, abuse, dysfunction, depression, and addiction.

All this emotional pain and turbulence is nothing more than a spiritual disconnect.

TO BE UNSHAKABLE

The tragic end of placing the need for beauty, acceptance, worth and love into the hands of others is emptiness. It is the evidence of soul abandonment, via spiritual starvation.

The struggle was, is, and forever will be, in connecting with Divinity. Discovering personal worth and value, and serving it to the world, comes no other way but by seeing yourself as an authentic expression, and radiant reflection, of the invisible One living on the inside of you.

Until the hidden is revealed, beauty isn't seen and truth goes unknown. Until light illuminates darkness, power forever evades. Until dead bones arise, glory will not cover the earth.

What needs resurrecting in your life?

Open your spiritual eyes and see yourself standing. Your feet are firmly planted, roots growing down deep, branches reaching for miles, and leaves abundant. Your thoughts are connected to heaven, your heart overflows with emotion and you are compelled to take inspired action daily.

Describe the action.

Now see yourself as water.

In a fluid state of grace-filled glory, you flow swiftly with great power! You turn, splash, crash, fill, nourish, cleanse, forge through mountains, make waves, purge, purify, refresh, and bring life to all you touch. You're unstoppable!

You are unstoppable in what? Is this helping or hurting you?

The power of you is hidden down deep in your spirit, serving as the anchor of your soul. This means that the stable, calm, confidence, that gloriously flows with soulful grace, to penetrate the hearts of all in its sphere, is IN you. It will not find it by looking to others.

CURRENT LOCATION?

Without knowing your current whereabouts, it is difficult to re-route, set sail and navigate your way to "Unshakable."

So where are you?

Call forth your spirit to arise and shine, and begin to connect with the love from which you came. It is in this homecoming that the call to intimacy is revealed. This is your mission.

As you enter in to this divine union, a clear mandate will arise from within, followed by a miraculous unveiling of YOU. The creator, the genius, the beauty, strength, power, wisdom and brilliance that you've always known was there, appears.

DEEP CALLS UNTO DEEP

An intimate knowing of the deep places within, happens through close encounters with the One who knits them all together. He has designed you to create an exquisite masterpiece with your life by first engraving the answers to life's big questions on the tablets of your heart.

So as you return to the problem of being tossed to and fro by the opinions of others, riding emotional roller coasters by sabotaging love and giving up your life to be accepted—by whom? May you find the simple solution of dancing with Divinity.

May you learn to embrace the practice of being still in order to know your great worth and exquisite beauty.

You are here to live abundantly and reflect divine beauty in all it's radiance. You are here to know grace and bring heaven to earth. You are here to experience glory in all its grandeur by delivering the gift of you. You are here to know love in all its fullness.

Press in, dig deep and discover, Unshakable You!

Living *Without* **Limitations**

Leta Russell

Leta is an in-demand Business Launch Expert, Coach, International Speaker and founder of Leta Russell International, LLC. Leta uses her expertise in mind mapping, strategic business planning, and 35 years of experience as an entrepreneur to help clients effortlessly break through confusion into clarity and action.

She lives back and forth between Portland, Oregon and Sydney, Australia where she enjoys an international lifestyle with her husband of 30 years, her best friend and #1 fan, Gil.

To access her free recording of the mind map webinar go to http:// mindmappingforbusiness.com

www.LetaRussell.com

f facebook.com/coachleta

○ twitter.com/letarussell

○ pinterest.com/letarussell/

in linkedin.com/in/letarussell

CHAPTER 12

MIND MAP YOUR VISION WITH PASSION AND POWER: CREATING CLARITY OUT OF CONFUSION

Leta Russell

Did you know that 67% of small business owners launch a business because of a personal passion? I'm not at all surprised, since I believe most entrepreneurs want to make a bigger difference and create a lifestyle doing the things they know, love, and find fulfillment from pursuing.

I and many of my clients fit into that 67% perfectly! I began my business because of a passion to help heart-centered entrepreneurs move through the maze of starting a business and launch with clarity and success…to help them Dream Big and Launch Bold. I saw how confused my clients were, in spite of their passion, enthusiasm, and talent. Because they felt overwhelmed, they were unable to take what they learned from many excellent courses and sources, map it into a strategic plan, and successfully launch and create enough money to keep going.

In the years of working with self-employed professionals and small business owners, helping them launch and reinvent their businesses, I have found these 3 key mistakes most impact their initial and long term financial success.

1. **Failure to identify a clear mission and vision for their business**

2. **Failure to establish a strong legal, financial, and sustainable business foundation**

3. **Failure to strategically plan a successful launch**

Having a clear, motivating, and inspired mission and vision will naturally attract the people who are perfectly served by your business. Intention drives success! Vision casting is simply communicating, in a big way, what you envision your business will look like into the future. It is key to creating a sustainable business and provides the fuel to power your dream when you face challenges. When you have a crystal clear and passionate vision you are unstoppable!

How do you go from being overwhelmed and confused to clarity? The first step I use with clients in designing the framework for their business vision may be something new to most readers. It's called Mind Mapping, and it is an excellent way to spark your imagination and Dream BIG!

Mind Mapping provides a new way to re-think, re-organize, and re-invent your business strategies to stand out in the current marketplace. By using every function of your brain along with visual clarity and stimulation, Mind Mapping provides the creative edge needed to succeed in today's economy.

Mind Mapping helps you create vivid images to trigger new ideas and help organize the chaos and confusion that often occurs in the planning or designing phase of a project. In short, it is the best tool I know of to break through overwhelm and into clarity.

WHAT IS A MIND MAP?

A Mind Map is a graphical way to represent ideas and concepts starting with a centralized theme. It is a visual creative tool that uses both the left and right brain to bring together analytical thinking with creative artistry, resulting in a richer, more engaging process of planning, organizing ideas and designing projects. Because of the radial design of a Mind Map, it tends to resemble the way the brain naturally functions, which enhances creativity, promotes clarity, sharpens focus, expands the mind, and provides a visual picture to work from.

The power of a Mind Map lies in its simplicity. The flexibility of a Mind Map lies in its many purposes in every area of our life, education and business. It can be used for simple everyday tasks, like "to do" lists, or something as complex as creating a comprehensive business plan, planning a major event, and creating applications, software, and products.

WHAT TO LOOK FOR IN MIND MAP TOOLS

There are some excellent digital tools available for the exercise. I personally prefer software that allows freehand drawing in vibrant colors, utilizes organic designs for creativity, and provides use of linear and grayscale options for a corporate look. I particularly enjoy brilliant color features that enhance creativity. I also appreciate the ability to collaborate with long distance clients on their Mind Maps; digital software allows us to share in their strategic planning process.

There are both paid and free open source software applications available. Most allow global collaboration and work with mobile applications, so explore and see what works best for you, your budget, and personal design preferences. Many paid software applications offer basic packages to get started and upgrades if you desire more options later.

You can also dive right into the process by using tangible tools like a large piece of paper or white board and colored markers. This is the perfect option if you tend to be technically challenged or just don't have the time to learn or budget for the digital software.

MIND MAPPING YOUR MISSION AND VISION

Start your Mind Map with your projected business name as the central idea and put as many action verbs as you can that represent your past and current strengths, talents, and natural gifts. Each word will be a branch off the central idea. Create a second map with "Ideal Client" as the central theme to brainstorm whom you want to reach. The third map called "Outcomes" will consist of the results you desire for your clients and your business.

As you begin each map, put every thought down and continue to work with it until a clear master plan begins to emerge. Feel free to edit or eliminate along the way, too. As you work on your big dream, ideas will come to you that you can add to the picture. In fact, that's the whole purpose of Mind Mapping—to create ideas and translate them into a simple, yet powerful, visual image.

You can use pictures, images, or words to convey an idea; in fact, mixing it up will promote even more creativity. Taking your ideas and communicating them into one or two words on a branch creates clarity. Trust me, your creative thought and intuition will be enhanced through the use of Mind Mapping!

From there, you'll create a mission statement that includes:

- **3 single action words** that describe or paint a picture of what you want to "do" in your business. (Choose the 3 most descriptive and powerful action words that stand out from your map.)
- **"Who"** the people are you want to reach with your message and service
- The **outcomes** or results you want to your clients to achieve.

Your mission statement will look something like this:

{Your Business Name} (3 action verbs) _____,
_____, _____ (who)
_____ to (what outcome) _____
_____.
(it can be more than one result)

Your vision simply expands that mission statement and defines the course for reaching your goals. Combine your mission with a picture of how you envision your company if it cannot fail, and use your Mind Mapping software (or by hand on a big sheet of paper), to create a simple "Vision" Mind Map that explores your purpose, values, and character. Include how you want people to feel when they do business with you, what products and services you intend to use to accomplish your mission. Provide a clear idea of the type of people you want to attract, and the results or benefits you want them to experience by working with you or buying from you.

You can use pictures, graphics, color, etc. to bring it alive. From that visual map, write a vision statement up to 3-4 paragraphs of what you want your company to be, do and have based on the points above. Keep it in the Present tense, be Specific, and be Descriptive.

Vision casting is a critical step to launching a business, yet it is one that many people skip or ignore. People get caught up in the everyday tasks of working "in" their business instead of working "on" their business and strategically planning for business success. In order to attract the perfect people, whether as clients or team members, creating and communicating a vision for your business future is essential to your long-term success in business.

Mind Mapping your vision with passion and power provides the visual map for setting and achieving goals, staying focused, communicating with your team and clients, as well as a destination that fuels enthusiasm and joy in your work. Clarity in your mission and vision is the compass that provides direction, keeps you on course, minimizes distractions, and eliminates overwhelm. Together they make a powerful team that sustains and builds profitability. As an added benefit, it makes what could be tedious and overwhelming a fun, creative process. It is the best way I know to break through chaos into clarity.

Are you ready to Mind Map your vision with passion and power? I'm offering a free webinar recording to help you get started with your BIG Dream. Check out my bio for a link to learn more.

Mike Gillespie

Mike Gillespie is a speaker, an author and a life coach who is driven to help others live their best life. He has had the privilege of coaching numerous individuals to create successful lives and careers. Through his coaching, online blog, and weekly "Start Me Up" newsletters, he inspires and motivates people to live more balanced and fulfilling lives overflowing with energy, happiness and purpose. He uses clear language and tools to empower clients to break free of their complacency and limiting beliefs, helping them clarify their goals to achieve maximum results. For a free life balance analysis, click

www.HappyHealthyandWise.me/Life-Balance.

www.MikeGillespie.com

www.HappyHealthyandWise.me

www.HelpaBillion.org

gplusid.com/MikeGillespie

✉ mike@HappyHealthyandWise.me

f facebook.com/mike.gillespie.718

f facebook.com/HappyHealthyandWise.me

𝕏 twitter.com/MikeGillespie88

⑨ youtube.com/user/MikeGillespie8

in ca.linkedin.com/in/mikegillespie8

CHAPTER 13

BALANCING LIFE – KEEP THE WHEELS OF LIFE TURNING

Mike Gillespie

Life can be bumpy if it's not in balance. I hear stories all the time about people who spend countless hours at their jobs making a lot of money, yet neglect their health and relationships. What's the point of being the richest person in the graveyard? Too often people are so obsessed with planning for the future that they forget to enjoy the moment and live in the now.

I have worked with countless individuals who are overwhelmed and unhappy despite being "successful" entrepreneurs or having high paying jobs. My clients range from those who say they can't stand their jobs and are feeling unfulfilled, to people who are not happy with their physical appearance and overall health. One of the biggest struggles I hear most from my clients is their desire to balance it all. Balance is defined as the ability to move or to remain in a position without losing control or falling. How is it possible for some people to maintain a healthy balance while others get overwhelmed and eventually burn out?

This question reminds me of one of my early coaching clients. He was a younger guy that wanted it all. When we first started working together, he was newly married with a newborn daughter, and working full time in a high paying job that was unfulfilling to him. On the surface, his issues did not sound overwhelming, but as we dug a little deeper, it was clear he had a lot on the go. On top of being a husband, a new dad, and working 40 hours at his day job, he also kept himself very busy with the multiple businesses that he was operating. Any free time that he had was quickly filled with business conferences or weekend workshops.

Once he got going, it was tough to slow him down. He seemed very proud of all he had on the go, almost as if it were a measure of success for him.

Throughout our earliest discussions, he attempted to justify his busy life and was very defensive about the choices he was making. When I asked him why he was busy all the time, he answered that it was for the future of his family. He believed all of his hard work now would provide him financial freedom that would offer more time for fun, family and fulfillment.

"Sounds like a nice future, but what's going on for you right now?"

"Are you close with your wife and new daughter?" I asked.

He hung his head and got quiet. From his silence, I sensed that was a no. I helped him to see the irony in that all of the things he was so busy with now were actually taking him further away from the things he said he wanted for his future.

"How would you feel living alone in a big empty house?"

I could tell that this was starting to get real for him and he got the point I was trying to make. He then uncrossed his arms, let his defenses down and asked for help.

He then asked me the question that I get all the time. "How do I make it all work?"

I reassured him that it's not as complicated as we often make it out to be.

The first step is awareness. Be honest with yourself by identifying your present situation. You can't get to where you want to go, if you don't know where you currently are.

I then introduced him to one of my favorite exercises. It is a very simple, yet powerful exercise called the Life Balance Wheel. More often than not, it is the simple things that offer the greatest results. In one quick glance, it shows a visual representation of your entire life. The rounder the wheel, the more balanced your life.

The Life Balance Wheel exercise is basically a circle divided up in to 8 Life Areas: Finances, Health, Profession, Family and Friends, Primary Relationship, Personal Development, Rest and Relaxation and Physical Surroundings.

Before we started in on the exercise, we talked about how he would define each category and which areas he was most struggling with. I then asked him to take a few minutes to rank his level of happiness and fulfillment for each life area with 1 being the lowest, and 10 being the highest. Once he had his rankings for all life areas, I had him draw a line that corresponded with the number, and asked him to shade in each life area.

We looked at his completed Life Balance Wheel together. He said it looked more like a star than a wheel. This is a common pattern I see when working with new clients. Looks pretty, but that's not what we are going for here. What I hear most from them are the difficulties maintaining a good work/life balance. I don't believe in work/life balance. It's just life. Work is just another area of your life. The Life Balance Wheel helps people see this. It's a small piece of the pie of life.

As we further analyzed his wheel, I asked him to picture it rolling along like a real wheel. He visualized the wheel moving along nicely and actually picking up speed when back-to-back life areas had similar rankings. It is comparable to a wheel rolling down a street with no stop signs. It maintains a good flow, while increasing momentum. On the other hand, he noticed a big slowdown in the wheel when one life area was an 8, and the next one was a 2. When the rankings bounce up and down like this, it's more like a windy road with potholes. It's next to impossible to get any real momentum. The wheel keeps trying to turn, but the pattern repeats unless something changes.

If you want something different, you have to do something different.

I looked at him and could tell from the look on his face that he was ready to do something different. With his newfound awareness, we could now work together and I could support him to bring more balance to his life.

I reminded him that the goal of this exercise was to have a better balance by having a round wheel. I recommend that all of my clients start out by evening out the life areas to make the wheel more round. The easiest way to do this is to shine a spotlight on the lowest ranked areas and then focus extra time and energy on them. Instead of having a bunch of 7s and 2s, work towards evening all life areas to around a 5. This will help minimize the ups and downs and get the wheel moving consistently.

Being low in one life area can drag down other life areas. Conversely, being high in one life area can lift up other life areas. More often than not, when you improve one life area, it will affect another life area. A quick way to round your wheel is to focus the majority of your efforts on improving the life areas that will positively impact multiple life areas. A good example of this is someone shifting out of an unfulfilling job. Finances may go down in the short term, but health, relationships, and physical surroundings would more than likely improve.

Once the life areas are evened out, it's time to start working towards increasing the rankings towards 10. The challenge is doing this in a balanced fashion. To overcome this challenge, track your progress by doing this exercise at least once every 3 months. It's no different than an athlete tracking their exercise routine or a company tracking their sales. The more frequently you do it, the quicker you can refocus your attention on the low ranked life areas.

If ever you feel a sense of overwhelm, focus on the 1% wins. Remember, small wins lead to big improvements over time. When you focus on one life area and you improve it by 1% each day for 30 days, you will see a 30% increase in that area of your life.

As you make progress, don't forget to celebrate along the way. Acknowledge yourself for the efforts you have already put in. It is a great reminder of how far you have come, and it helps to keep the motivation levels high.

Life balance is not a destination; it is an ongoing work in progress. The more you work at it, the better it will be.

I am driven by helping people live better lives. My clients have had major shifts in their perspectives because I have encouraged them to look at things differently. When they have their inevitable ups and downs, I am there to support them and get them back on track quickly. This is why having a coach is so valuable.

Today is the first day of the rest of your life. Start living your best life today.

Michael Hanle

Michael Hanle is Owner and CEO of Guidance to Greatness Personal Empowerment Services providing coaching and consulting services that encompass a Mind, Body, Soul—"Whole Life" philosophy. Michael is a member of the International Coaching Federation (ICF), a Gallup-Certified Strengths Coach, Personal Empowerment Coach and Marketing Plan Coach/Consultant. He boasts over 10 years of corporate business leadership, marketing and sales knowledge with The Ritz-Carlton Development Company, with expertise and awards in areas of team building, strengths-based personal development and strategic marketing plan design.

Explore available coaching programs or subscribe to Michael's "Great Blog":

www.GuidancetoGreatness.com

f **facebook.com/G2GCoaching**

◯ **twitter.com/G2GCoaching**

in **linkedin.com/pub/Michael-Hanle/18/445/523/**

CHAPTER 14

CHANGE IS GONNA COME: STOP DREADING AND START HARNESSING ITS POWER!

Michael Hanle

> We all have a unique gift to give this world and your gift lies within your greatness; don't keep the world waiting any longer!
>
> **Michael Hanle**

"I hate Change!" "Change is tough!" "I am not good with change!" How many of us have said one or all of these statements at some point in our lives? It is the most common theme I deal with in my coaching practice by far! Yes, there are times when we do accept change, when we can actually see that certain change in our lives is a good thing. But for our purpose here, let's focus on the "not-so-good" type of change that I help my clients navigate through on a daily basis, shall we?

We have all had those moments when it seems everything comes crashing down at once all around us. In fact, it seems like it happens in waves doesn't it? A period of time when not only just in our life, but everyone you seem to talk to has some type of major change happening in his or her life that feels huge or insurmountable. We often sink into a helpless place during these times. It is very easy to do, especially if we give in to the notion that we have no control over the situation, and it's completely out of our hands, and we are just surrounded by or destined for doom and gloom. This is the pivotal point where I have seen coaching work miracles.

It is at this point that I normally share a fundamental principle of Guidance to Greatness Personal Empowerment Services, the point where I propose a radical new way of thinking to my clients about the (often) dreaded word "change." If used properly, any change, even change that seems negative and life altering, can actually be the kindling and initial spark for what I've deemed as our Personal T&T™, that when combined with a few other layers and means of introspection can ignite and unearth greatness within us that has the power to transform our world as we know it.

Let's have some fun now and imagine that we are actually in a session together on this topic of negative change, shall we?

Going back to our initial conversation, is it true for you that the experiences that come along with what you've perceived as "negative" change really do happen in waves of sheer coincidence, bad luck, jinxed JuJu? Or, could it be that there is something else working here— something that instead of being against you is actually there FOR you to use as a "navigational system" of sorts? Could it be? Could there be a "wonderful" and universal law of attraction that is merely bringing in repeated experiences or people to your life experiencing the same things you are because very simply put; they are a match to what you are "vibrating in that moment?"

Going a step further, if you think back on your life and a moment when you thought the world would end or your life would never recover but it did and you did; what can you learn from that experience? If you could go back and follow the patterns of your thoughts and actions at the time of that major change that you have now "recovered" from, would it be true for you to say that you actually used the experience to get clearer on what you did not want in your life? Did it eventually (depending on how long you allowed yourself to hold on and resisted the change) turn into clear powerful thoughts and desires of what you DID want in your life? Isn't it true that as soon as you let go of what I like to call the transition part of the change and you stopped resisting, the transformation happened—by way of your new thoughts, your new vibration or better put, "your new point of attraction?" How amazing is it that all this happened without your conscious effort? Can you imagine what you could create or where your life could go if you were conscious through all of this?

If you allow yourself to think in this direction for just a moment, what does it do for you? Does it open up for you the powerful possibility that maybe, just maybe, you have some control over the outcome of your current situation after all? With what we have covered here, can you agree that it really comes down to the thoughts you are thinking? If I can summarize, what we have said here is that your thoughts are merely energy that controls the vibration you are putting "out there," vibration that is actually attracting this "jinxed juju" you are experiencing at the moment. So what is stopping you from changing that vibration simply by changing your thoughts about it?! Or better yet, harnessing the energy in this HUGE change in your life and using it to catapult you to a new bigger, better, GREATER place of being!

With that said then, it's become obvious that your first step is shifting your mind, your thoughts, your feeling place about this change that you are currently defining as negative, correct? Let's do an exercise to help you do that. Regardless of where your beliefs lie on this subject, I encourage you to try the simple exercise below that I utilize with my coaching clients (and myself!) when dealing with "negative" change:

- Stop with the commiserating with everyone going through the same thing you are! Think: Is this activity bringing me a feeling of joy or lightheartedness in any way? If not, well YOU ARE GOING THE WRONG WAY!

- Close your eyes and go back to an experience in your life that surprised the crap out of you. A time when something or someone incredible appeared in your life, seemingly right out of thin air that literally changed your life—even just a little bit. Are you there?

- Next ask yourself if that is possible again? If it happened then, why couldn't it happen now? You didn't expect it back then did you? You don't have to know exactly what it will be or what it looks like, in fact you probably won't. Sit with that for a moment. Can you feel yourself opening to the possibilties, even a little twinge of excitement? Let that feeling marinate for a few minutes.

- Now go "general!" Going with your new premise that anything is possible, without going too specific into the issue you are dealing with, open your mind and the space for this new way of thinking by **feeling** how all this feels for you. What general emotions do you want to feel? Use the five senses, what does the end result smell, taste, sound, and feel like? Have fun with this for a little while and let yourself bask in the feeling of it.

- Go pet your dog! :) Seriously, go do anything you can to put yourself in a good feeling place—a movie, a walk, a blooper reel, dancing, music. Whatever it is that gets you there, go do it now!

The basic premise with all this and that I have found to be true for my clients and myself is that we (I included) have to open ourselves up to the change that we want to see by first creating the space for it in our mind, truly feeling it and then letting the universe do the rest. It is not any of our business to know how it is supposed to happen or what exactly it is supposed to look like. ALL that matters is that we know the general FEELING we want to feel in the end, even if that is simply relief by accepting the change so we can then work from there.

By doing this simple exercise my clients have gained more of a feeling or realization that they DO have a choice in all of this. A choice to not just accept change, but embrace it or, dare I say, a sense of excitement to USE it to ignite the greatness that lies within them that is waiting to be expressed! There is nothing stopping you from doing the same!

As I reflect on what I have seen with my clients and even times in my own life that I was most at peace and happy, it is when we are not trying to orchestrate every little detail of life, but rather trusting in the flow. Undoubtedly some changes are easier to navigate than others, but I am happy to say I am learning to be more deliberate these days when it comes to this particular paradigm, and it feels empowering indeed! It is from this place that I draw my love for coaching, write this chapter and ultimately what I hope it brings to each and every one of you.... Aloha.

Krista VonWiller

Krista is a native San Diegan who relocated with her beloved Husband and Son to Tulsa, OK. With ten plus years as a Certified Human Resources Professional, Krista left her full-time job to become a stay-at-home parent. Talk about a humbling experience. Prior to uprooting the world she had known for over a decade, Krista became a Certified Massage Therapist in California and moved her mobile massage business to the Tulsa area. From there she developed into and studied to be a Life Coach. One of her many life passions is connection—with others and with self.

Phone: 619-985-8713
Town: Tulsa, Oklahoma

www.massagekneadsyou.com

Skype: krista.vonwiller

massagekneadsyou@yahoo.com

facebook.com/kvonwiller

facebook.com/massagekneadsyou

facebook.com/pages/Life-Massage/350895955017100

CHAPTER 15

DEALING WITH PRICKLY PERSONALITIES

Krista VonWiller

Spiky. Spiny. Thorny. Barbed.

Just a few synonyms to alternately describe prickly. Take your time in imagining an unsettling experience that you have encountered with a co-worker. Did you overhear someone speaking in a horrible way and assume it was about you—only to find out later that what you thought was the case, in actuality, was something completely different?

Have you ever reveled in the clarity of realizing that the *object* of your obsession and their prickly ways didn't have anything to do with you at all? "Wow! I'm so relieved. It *really* wasn't ME."

In thinking back, have you ever encountered someone that "rubbed you the wrong way?" Or maybe, you have experienced someone that was intentionally directing their *not so feel-good* energy at you. Regardless of circumstance, these encounters feel upside down and, in some cases, devastating.

Your working role takes on quite a life, doesn't it? You spend HOURS of your life performing a job in a capacity that lacks passion. You do it to earn a living. You do it to fit in. To feel successful. Hopefully you are doing what you love during your one valuable life. Hopefully the people that you are doing it with are enjoyable...across the board. Hopefully you are on the same wavelength with everyone in your life, both professionally and personally.

But if you're not at that place in your life now, or maybe you previously have been, or if you feel that it could ever be possible to encounter this type of individual at possibly some point in your life, then I humbly suggest finishing this chapter.

Ask yourself, "Am I ready to deal with myself in moving past these feelings of upset, frustration and (possibly) anger?" I coach my clients in a moment like this to reframe. Consider instead, "I AM ready to deal with myself in moving past these feelings..."

Clients have described their working environment as "toxic." Poisonous. Deadly. Lethal. Contaminated. Are you comfortable in honoring the honesty in your choice of adjective? It appears to be common to brush it off and keep going because, "I really need my job." The undertaking, however, of said "job" is quite a personal sacrifice.

From the office politics to the sometimes slanderous and defamatory conversations in the break room, there are seemingly no boundaries.

How does one mix the personal with the professional anyway? Many of my clients talk about enjoying the opportunity to make connections in the work place. That is a fairly big grey area, especially when those "personal" connections are made with a superior, subordinate or a department co-worker.

Some clients have had the comfort, or lack thereof, in working with the SAME people for upwards of 30 years. Current and former clients alike describe an experience of working with someone that they considered a friend and then one day it all changed. Their *friend* had changed. And through those coaching sessions my clients realized that they had changed as well and had become their own version of the prickly perpetrator. Ultimately these clients were able to see, for themselves, that they did not understand what their befriended co-worker was going through nor did they take time to reach out to inquire.

As a Life Coach, I will facilitate a safe space for you to move past the dismay of these issues. It can be of benefit to try stepping out of your state of repeated complaints and curiosity. You know that life has its way of changing unexpectedly and sometimes you chalk up that change to "it is what it is." I coach clients to speak with that person that they once shared a strong bond with. WHY NOT take a moment to dispel the wondering?!

Some breakthrough clients have spent years under the verbal beat-down thumb of their boss and other workplace figures of authority. They suffered emotionally and physically from the stress and the anguish of knowing that they had to return each day to hell. They have spoken of loving their job and therefore chose to endure the daily grind of articulated torture.

From the coaching process, clients began discovering new sides to their respective unrelenting leader and were finally able to stand back from the "stuckness" of the experience to realize that it only felt bad when the clients allowed it to. Meaning, once the clients stopped taking the prickly interactions personally, they were able to see their superiors/bosses differently, and safely separate themselves from the ongoing anguish. More importantly, clients were able to see *themselves* differently, which allowed them to finally move beyond the torment.

A common occurrence affecting many of my clients is introversion. These clients are the type of individual that mostly keep to themselves while at work. With the limited interaction came varying moments of loneliness during their workday/shift. These clients expressed interest in learning how to engage more comfortably with those that *appeared* to "have it all together." Some of these clients described instantly freezing when in the mere presence of certain individuals in the workplace. And, in turn, described feeling like they were getting the "cold shoulder."

Following many sessions, the breakthrough moments came when these clients were alone with the "confident" co-worker and decided to initiate a conversation. Interestingly, it turned out that the co-worker thought that the client was conceited/full of themselves… essentially the mirror of the other. At this point of revelation clients described having feelings of relief and disbelief. At the end of it all, it is hard to believe that such strife can come from utterly nothing more than a simple misunderstanding.

Sometimes it is the work itself that creates prickly perilous politics in the workplace. Many times I coach clients into stepping up and creating an opportunity to speak with the "offender." Of course, it is not uncommon to receive a response of, "I'm not comfortable with that." I remind my clients that while at work, unless self-employed, you are playing someone else's game. If you can master the rules, you stand a great chance of experiencing smooth sailing. Of course, as you have read, there may always be others in the vicinity of your employ that may not make it such a great place to work.

Coaching clients in this way, to create a positive workplace for themselves, is a tough love approach that allows them to see that they have a choice in how to step through these uncomfortable situations.

My clients vary in age, from adolescent to elderly. There is not a magic number in life that sets you free from the impact of others. There is, on the other hand, awareness. Developing the ability to safely receive a perceived prickly offering. Knowing how to protect yourself while receiving the other person's energy (e.g., via sight and/or sound, in writing, etc.).

However the pot shot arrives, I am able to coach you beyond the chaos of living in and creating your own prickly life. Anyone is susceptible; the question is: how do you *feel* about it and what are YOU doing to change it?

Clients close to coaching completion are reportedly able to sense a sensation within their body* immediately. The beauty of my clients' successes: identify the trigger and *let it go.*

Please consider: **Are you fulfilled?** Are you satisfied with the way in which you earn your money? Are YOU at peace with how you are spending hours of your precious time? Are you calm and at peace with this variable of your life known as "work?"

If any of your answers are 'no,' then it is a great time…a perfect time… in your life to figure out how to get yourself there. Steps forward will come. Be brave. Have courage. Expect pain (e.g., emotional, physical). Know that change happens, hurts and then heals.

---

* Advanced clients have described feeling their reaction to prickly situations within their bodies (e.g., stomach & upper/lower chest).

Coaching is an effective and, at times, fast-acting method to move you beyond your workplace suffering. The recipe for personal success is simple and very sweet. You, along with your coach, are the main ingredients to creating an empowered and undisturbed workplace experience. I look forward to our connection.

Shannon Staples

Shannon Staples is a Certified Life Coach and Energy Therapist creating her own passion-filled career as the owner of High Vitality Life. Her passion for personal growth and helping others has resulted in an avid interest in the Law of Attraction and Energy Medicine of all kinds, as well as certifications in Counseling, NLP, and Hypnotherapy. Shannon works with clients worldwide to realize her mission of raising the world's vibration by creating a critical mass of joyful individuals.

www.highvitalitylife.com

Skype ID: sdstaples

plus.google.com/108048653260274545153

✉ shannon@highvitalitylife.com

❶ facebook.com/highvitalitylife

Ⓟ pinterest.com/sdstaples1

▶ youtube.com/user/sdstaples

ⓘⓃ ca.linkedin.com/in/shannonstaples/

CHAPTER 16

TRANSFORMING THE ENERGY OF YOUR SUBCONSCIOUS PROGRAMMING

Shannon Staples

As a Life Coach and Energy Therapist, I find my clients often struggle with subconscious blocks. With the best of intentions, they may work hard and take action but still find themselves falling back into the same old patterns. Let's talk about how you can get to the root cause of your issues and transform your energetic patterns – and your life – forever.

Patterns are like habits, but most are entirely unconscious. You may not even know that you are creating certain patterns of behaviour that may be contributing to you feeling stuck. At the core of this problem is simply blocked energy and subconscious programming.

Energy plays an integral role in the patterns you create. Quantum mechanics tells us everything is energy. Whether you look at a chair, a rock, or your skin under a microscope, the subatomic level contains mostly empty space, which holds the energy of light, information and possibility. You may have heard it called the zero point, the God space, or the universal force.

This energy is in everything and affects all areas of our lives, spiritually, mentally, emotionally and physically. Energy – including information, thoughts and beliefs – flows by vibrational frequencies that cannot be seen. Just like TVs, satellites and cell phones, our bodies act as transmitters and receivers of electromagnetic energy waves, which resonate or attract things with a compatible vibration.

The subconscious mind uses the information of every life experience to create your self-image and belief system. As you go through life, everything you experience is filtered through the subconscious programming, which directs how you react. The subconscious is where patterns and blocks develop.

You might be wondering, if these blocks are subconscious, how do we find and change them? There are hundreds of different methods for transforming or overcoming this subconscious programming, such as coaching, psychotherapy, meditation, journaling, art, affirmations, brain entrainment, hypnosis, subliminal messages, energy healing, releasing emotions, raising your vibration and changing your patterns, to name a few. I use several of these to help my clients, especially those that are based in energy transformation.

There are three main ways I have found to shift subconscious programming:

1. Analysis
2. Rewiring your brain
3. Energy therapy

Any of these can be used in conjunction with others to get more rapid results. Let's look at each and you can decide what resonates best for you.

Analysis: This might include things like psychotherapy, coaching, hypnotherapy, or journaling. This is the part, as a Life Coach, where I help you dig deep, explore the possible sources of a problem, analyze it and use this new information to understand, heal and grow.

- If you could read the information stored in your subconscious mind, what do you think you would find in the file called *limiting beliefs?*
- Where in your life experiences database, do you think they developed?
- What hidden or obvious benefits do you think they were designed for?
- Are they still useful?

Analysis is certainly helpful for clarity and understanding and can also contribute to releasing blocks by bringing them to your conscious awareness. I find it works best for my clients when combined with some of the other methods.

Have you achieved your desired result by using analysis in the past? Whether you did or not, keep in mind that subconscious programs will often recur if you didn't deal with it at the subconscious, energetic level. You need to shift or release the underlying energy of those unconscious ideas so the outdated belief system can dissolve. Releasing the root of the issue may not be possible through analysis alone because thinking is done in your conscious mind, which only contains about 10-20% of your manifesting power, whereas the subconscious mind holds 80-90%.

Rewire Your Brain: Since you can't think or reason with the subconscious mind, it is obviously trickier to change. One way to transform your subconscious programming is through brain plasticity. The more you practice or repeat certain thoughts and behaviours, the stronger that neural pathway becomes and the easier it is to do the task without consciously thinking about it. For example when you first learn to drive you have to think about every little thing you are doing, but eventually these *repeated actions* form such strong neural pathways that it filters down into the subconscious until we can drive from one end of town to the other on autopilot. Sometimes we don't even remember what happened between leaving home and arriving at our destination!

There are some amazing technologies to help speed this learning process up, such as brain entrainment and subliminal messages, as well as some lower tech methods like hypnosis, reciting affirmations and using a vision board. I have found these methods to be most successful if you engage your emotions, which have more energetic power than thoughts alone.

Another way to rewire your brain is by observing and changing the patterns that repeat in multiple areas of your life. This is a very practical and simple method – though not always easy – to transform your energy blocks and live in the flow. It only requires an open mind to recognize the patterns, and a desire to make changes.

Discovering your patterns is as easy as noticing similarities in the kinds of people you attract and experiences you create.

- Take a look around at your house, office, friends, family (especially your parents), relationships, attitudes and emotions. Can you find any emerging patterns?

For example many of my clients find that *clutter* is a repeating pattern – in their house, in their mind, in their business, and in their parents' lives. They often experience it in different areas of their life as messiness, feeling unsure, lack of confidence, scattered thinking, or feeling overloaded because they have a pattern of *disorganization*.

Another way to look for patterns is to first think about how you feel and then see how it manifests. For example, being *overwhelmed* is another common issue I see.

- Are you involved in too many projects or activities; do you eat when you're not hungry; are your cupboards and bookshelves bursting with stuff?
- If so, ask yourself where else in your life are you full to the brim, and seeking more?
- Maybe you are full in terms of information, time, effort, emotions, or relationships?
- Is your excess space all used up?

This will reduce the flow of energy in your life and result in blocks such as feeling like you can't do things, you don't know enough, aren't smart enough, aren't loved enough, or you create some other drama because you have a pattern of always *needing more*.

- What new behaviour would you like to create to overwrite the old pattern in just one area of your life?
- What specific steps can you take to implement this new habit?
- What might get in the way of it?
- What resources do you have to overcome the obstacles in your plan?

Continuing on with the examples above, you will find that by simply removing the excess stuff from your house, you are breaking the old pattern and creating a new one that allows energy to flow. However, you must be careful to keep from falling back into the old pattern and continue to find and change more patterns where you can. This one simple change will affect your work life, your personal life and your spiritual life in surprising ways. It's important to celebrate the changes you create in your inner and outer world and remain mindful of what you learn to make this process more gratifying.

Energy Therapy: Since we are vibrational beings, it makes sense to deal with our issues at the deepest possible level – energy. Once you find and shift the underlying energy from blocked to flowing, or from a lower vibration to a higher vibration, the subconscious program or pattern is transformed permanently.

There are hundreds of different energy therapy modalities and many are very simple to learn and implement yourself. I have found energy healing to be fast and easy to learn. I often teach my clients some basics so they can help themselves between sessions to keep moving forward.

Remember that what you see in the world around you is a reflection of your beliefs and self-image. If you don't like what you see out there, then it's time to look at your internal programming to discover why you are attracting this into your life. Dig deep, discover hidden benefits, observe patterns, change behaviours and transform your energy to overcome the subconscious programming that is thwarting your plans to create your ideal life!

Rebecca David

Rebecca is a certified Life & Health Coach at Rebecca David, LLC and a holistic remedy enthusiast! Rebecca is a passionate entrepreneurial woman always seeking to learn and inspire others to live their life in a healthy vibrant way full of gratitude and pursuing their unique gifts & talents!

www.rebeccadavid.com

Skype: meetrebeccadavid

f **facebook.com/RebeccaDavidOnline**

twitter.com/rebeccadavid

youtube.com/rebeccadavidtv

linkedin.com/in/sweetspirit

CHAPTER 17

EXPOSE AND EMPOWER YOUR GIFTS AND TALENTS
Rebecca David

It's such a joy and honor to witness the passion and life come forward in someone during our coaching sessions when they begin to truly believe and explore the reality of living a fulfilled life, one that allows them to live in a way that fully expresses their unique gifts and talents!

I have spoken with hundreds of people who seem rather void of passion, who are not feeling fulfilled in their life. I can assure you that remarkable transformation begins to unfold as they trust the coaching process, and begin to express their gifts or talents that lie within them waiting to be fulfilled. Suddenly an excitement and passion rises in their voice, there is energy of anticipation and a desire to bring about that which they were created to do!

- What do you love to do?
- What's fun for you?
- What is it you long for?

Many are going through life void of passion and unfulfilled in life's journey, yet often all it takes is a trusted, committed coaching partnership offering them the opportunity to be heard; a partnership of accountability so they can achieve their goals. This can bring about the shifts leading to a transformed life, where they are truly alive and contributing their gifts and talents, making a positive difference in their life as well as the lives of many others.

My clients desire to be brave or bold enough to break free of the routine and self-imposed limitations so they can express their magnificence within and create a life truly worth living allowing them to life a healthy & vibrant life. Our coaching partnership offers them a safe space to speak of their gifts and talents, and accountability to pursue the goals they set. Then they can live an authentic life of using their gifts and talents in a way that is personally and financially fulfilling, making a positive difference in their life and the lives of many.

- What gift or talent lies with you, longing to be exposed and empowered?
- What can you do for hours and enjoy?
- What inspires you?

I truly believe we are each created on purpose and for a purpose. We have gifts and talents within us that often are not nurtured fully; they are kept hidden and therefore not benefiting us or anyone else. Not pursuing your gift or talent will often leave a deep void within, a longing that nothing else seems to fill. It can also and often does lead to illness.

As a holistic life coach I have witnessed so many people living in despair with unhealthy lives. You were created to thrive and make manifest the gifts and talents placed within you. When you don't honor that by ignoring it or playing small or insignificant, it creates a dissatisfaction within that often leads to an illness due to your authentic self being suppressed. The illness often tells the story of unfulfilled potential. Until you are able to expose the gifts and talents within, and empower them by cultivating them to fruition you will not be fulfilled, and that lack of fulfillment usually leads to an unhealthy life.

This chapter was written specifically for you, the one with the longing inside for something different, the one who knows you were created for more than you have going on in your life currently.

Some say we come into this world as an empty vessel, knowing nothing. I say we come into this world on purpose, for a purpose and with unique precious gifts & talents chosen specifically for us.

- How do you feel when you are fully engaged in your gift/talent?
- What is one thing that is stopping you from fully using your gift/talent?
- Is this a Limiting belief or a truth?

Some clients have expressed concerns that pursuing their gifts and talents may seem self-gratifying. On the contrary, fulfilling your inner desire to live out your unique gifts and talents is actually honoring and selfless, to pursue that which is calling you. Through coaching, my clients are able to embrace fully their unique calling and bring forth their gifts and talents. They can begin living a life they truly are excited about, one that is fulfilling in many ways.

- What gives you a feeling of fulfillment and a desire to do more?
- What would you rather do with your time that you are not currently doing?
- What would you do even if you didn't earn money doing it?

I love the analogy of the garden; let's call your unique gift or talent a seed. The seed holds within it amazing potential to become what it was created to become, but only when nurtured and cultivated properly. When the seed is properly nourished and nurtured, it breaks open to produce something much greater than itself, something that contains more seed, giving it the ability to continually produce.

Just like us—we have seeds (gifts and talents) within that when cultivated, nurtured and nourished properly brings about much greater than its original seed.

- Other than yourself, who will best benefit by your exposing and empowering your gifts and talents?

It's such an unselfish thing to pursue, for the benefits are far reaching, more than you could be aware of. The gifts and talents were placed within you because you are the one who is capable of achieving them. By doing so, you will not only blossom and live your best life; you will touch the lives of others and therefore positively change many other lives as well. You have the ability to reach and impact many people that others may not be able to reach.

- What is it that allows you to feel more alive, more excited about the life you've been given?
- Are you currently using your gifts or talents in a way that brings a great sense of fulfillment within you?
- Describe how you will feel when you begin to use your gifts and talents and you are actually earning a great income doing so.

"Exposing" Your Talents and Gifts indicates they are hidden, already within you. "Empowering" them is to bring them forth to make a positive difference for you and others!

- What is one thing that is stopping you from fully pursuing your gift/talent?
- What is one thing you will do today to move you toward fulfilling this?

Action will take you out of doubt and doubt will take you out of action.

You are an extraordinary person!

While you are here, you have an opportunity to grow, contribute, and make a positive difference in your life and in the lives of others.

As long as breath remains within you, you have an opportunity to change things up; to live with more joy, more passion and more engagement; to feel the vibrancy that lies dormant within you! There is a way and it's an exciting journey to discover it!

- Is it time for you to actually live fully the life you've been given and bring out the gift within you that just needs to be cultivated?

If questions or doubts come up, as they do for many, begin to ask yourself empowering questions. Questions such as "How can I?" "What is one thing I can do today to bring me closer to my goal?"

Find ways to make it happen rather than finding ways to be defeated.

Change your perspective to an empowering one that inspires you!

You've got all the answers already!

Are you ready to break free of whatever is holding you back from fully exposing your gifts and talents, so you can empower them to benefit the lives of many? You know you have a mission to fulfill; let's partner together and make it happen!

I am here ready to partner with you as your Coach to help you reach each goal along the way bringing you closer to living your authentic congruent life, where your everyday actions are a reflection of your unique gifts and talents.

It is certainly a privilege and an honor to work with you on this important mission that will definitely make a positive difference in your life, and also have an enormous ripple effect of positive change in the world we live in.

Let's begin…

Empowering you to live a healthy vibrant life!

Hazel Moore

Hazel Moore currently lives in England, and is the founder of Spiritual Mastery, with 30 years' experience behind her. Holding certificates in counselling from the University of Canterbury, diplomas in spiritual life coaching, motivational speaking, teaching and mentoring, she has become an expert in coaching people to bring about powerful inner shifts that lead to success, abundance and personal happiness. Her vision for her business is to bring her passion and joy, with her unique talents, to as many people as possible using her entrepreneurial skills on a global level through the internet.

www.hazelmoore.yolasite.com

www.hazelmoore.net

✉ **thankyou.universe@btinternet.com**

✉ **hellohazel@btinternet.com**

f **facebook.com/HazelMooreSpiritualMastery**

𝕏 **twitter.com/MyMagicLife9**

in **linkedin.com/in/hazelmoorespiritualmastery**

CHAPTER 18

OUT OF YOUR MIND AND INTO YOUR HEART
MENTAL AND EMOTIONAL MASTERY
Hazel Moore

As an intuitive life coach I have discovered that many of my clients have felt that their Life is one big struggle, a constant feeling of swimming upstream or of being trapped in a cage that they don't know how to get out of, let alone how they got into it.

They expressed concerns to me that they didn't know the way forward out of the chaos and turbulent thoughts and emotions which often rendered them paralyzed, exhausted and in a constant state of kneejerk reactions to people and events around them.

I always tell them that the first important step is to set the intention that struggle is not an option any longer, neither is lack or conflict in any shape or form. That it's time to understand, know and own beyond a shadow of a doubt, that Life should flow easily, downstream, and was always meant to work in their favor. You are meant to be successful, abundant, free and full of joy and there is a place inside you where the means to create this in your Life is found. This place is your Heart and all that is necessary is for you to step out of your Mind and back into your Heart.

Your Mind is made up of your thoughts and your emotions. Emotions are feelings that flow from the Heart, and are felt in the body as a movement of energy and this creates what we call moods. Thoughts and emotions bounce off one another, like a ping pong ball going back and forth from one bat to the other and, according to the quality of that thought and emotion is what the outcome of how you feel at any given moment will be, what mood you are experiencing. Many of my clients have had a pretty low set point with their feelings, ranging from boredom and frustration through to sadness, apathy, lack, anger, rage, numbness and feeling "less than."

To own such feelings can be a scary, overwhelming experience but it doesn't have to be that way. It will be amazing to you how quickly such powerful and deep feelings of despair, sadness and anger can be transmuted into peace with the techniques I use.

The energy of your powerful emotions is triggered by your reaction to your thoughts or external trauma, and unless it is dealt with and released, it will remain in your aura. This can cause a heavy feeling in you, until the next time it is triggered, usually by somebody "pressing your buttons." This in turn causes a never-ending cycle, because you will continue, by the Law of Attraction, to magnetize these triggers to you. Old painful memories coming to Mind will also trigger your numbed emotions. This happens because the energy of that emotion is already in you; it is not something that someone else has caused or put there. And until you heal that emotion by embracing it, it will remain within you.

Years pass, lifetimes pass and we forget the event or the thoughts that created the original emotion, and yet because of them lying dormant, we are still triggered. Not only that, more negative emotion has been left unexpressed in our aura, all piling up, just sitting there waiting to be triggered. It results in intensifying the very emotions and moods that we want to heal because they are controlling our lives.

I would like to put a question to you. But before I do, can I ask you to close your eyes for a moment, put your hand on your Heart and allow yourself to feel the deepest feelings that reside there, and ask yourself, "Can I, am I prepared to live in the way I have been relating to myself and the world for the next 10, 20 years or more?"

With your hand remaining on your Heart watch the thoughts and then the emotions that that life changing question brings up in you. Watch the reactions that are present in your body as you continue to feel your way through the question. Don't engage your thinking in this process, just allow the emotion to be what it is, to rise up in you so that you can embrace it. Yes, embrace it, welcome it. Say to it,

"Welcome," don't push it away. Let it be there and in your mind see a door opening into it and walk through the door. After a moment ask it if it has something to show you or tell you or is ready to leave. You will be astonished to find that you will receive an answer. That answer may come in the form of a positive feeling, thoughts in your head or as a picture. Let it come to you; don't force anything, remember your Heart is in control and your Heart knows what is best for you and wants what is best for you. If you get frustrated leave it alone and go back to the technique later.

As you continue to practice this and interact from your Heart with your emotions, you will come to realize how all of your pent up feelings have needed to be heard, expressed, forgiven and released. A practice that all of my clients are very familiar with is to say to their emotions, "I love you, forgive me, I'm sorry," and they repeat this until the emotion is ready to leave their aura. When it leaves, they tell me that there is a powerful sense of release and gratitude resulting in a feeling of lightness, like a balloon drifting gently away on the wings of a breeze.

Everything can change in a moment when we set a strong intention and realize perhaps for the first time that our Mind, our thoughts and emotions, are inseparable from our physical body and Heart. They are all linked together by buffers of layers of consciousness: mental, emotional and spiritual intelligence. Your Mind is just one part of your soul, and as such is a link, a buffer, between your Heart and your body. The buck stops with the body, and if you stay in that relentless game of Mind, of bat and ball, the good opportunities are often stacked against you, and your body will bear the brunt of those mind games, showing up eventually as illness, chaos and lack in your Life. Everything you are not in truth about, have not expressed, will appear as a block either in your body or your Life.

As you continue to work with your Heart feelings by asking your Heart the very questions that you would normally ask other people, more of your Sacred Truth will become apparent and over time your thought patterns will change. And because you yearn for that change you will attract to yourself people, events, books and new ways of thinking that will impact your emotions in a very positive joyful way.

This in turn will lead you on to even more important and powerful discoveries about yourself and how multi-dimensional you are.

The teachings and techniques that I have to share with you will change the vibration of you, which in turn will change the dynamics of your family and your circumstances, and that will lead to global change. It works like this. Desire and fear form a pair of opposites and each has an electromagnetic pull, a powerful force, which in turn creates a feeling of conflict within you. Desire pulls something toward you, and fear pushes it away from you. This is the Mind at work with its home in duality. That's what it knows. It feels completely separate from the Heart and has us believing that's all that we are, that that is our lot, so at best accept it, and at worst fight it all the way. This is polarity consciousness, division, at work again, and a house divided falls apart.

It can and does take years to figure all this out and when you have figured it out, still from the same place of your Mind, what then? Well, everything carries on just the same, because the emotional energy has not been released from your auric field; and your thoughts cannot improve, because the emotional baggage is holding them stuck. It's a double whammy.

Living from your Heart opens you to an awareness within you that watches all the dramas in your Life with no opinion, no judgment, no conflict. This awareness is Love; and it is this power that changes everything, so that you can show up as the best you that you can be.

As an intuitive life coach it is my passion and my joy to watch my clients' transition into something beautiful, like the caterpillar turning into a butterfly. As their coach and mentor I feel very privileged to watch them become more than they were before and step into being powerful, successful, loving people.

Faith J. Dugan

Faith Dugan, M.P.A. has over 20 years of accounting experience in private, non-profit, and government sectors, managing multi-million dollar budgets. She holds a bachelor's degree in accounting and management, as well as a master's degree in public administration. Her life purpose is to mentor and inspire others to become financially empowered, by turning financial overwhelm into financial mastery, thus attracting wealth. She teaches money mastery techniques, sets up financial structures, and helps free others from bondage beliefs keeping them a slave to money.

www.askthemoneymentor.com

f facebook.com/faithjdugan

f facebook.com/themoneymentor

y twitter.com/askmoneymentor

p pinterest.com/themoneymentor

in linkedin.com/in/faithduganmpa

123

CHAPTER 19

MONEY MASTERY IS YOUR KEY TO PROSPERITY

Faith Dugan

How can we *live without limitations* when we don't feel prosperous? Many of my clients feel prosperity is unattainable at times. Not surprising, as many have been raised by well-meaning adults verbalizing their own fears of money, meaning to prepare them for the "real world." Instead of preparation, they passed on fear of money, which creates resistance and pushes money away. Many fear-based beliefs are created when you feel you don't deserve money or it's sinful to desire money. Others are afraid of rejection from friends and family members; or feel you're taking from others if you're prosperous. Have you ever noticed the more you *chase* money, the more elusive money becomes? If you struggle with these fear-based limiting beliefs, you will struggle with money until you change your perception from money slavery to money mastery.

If you do *not* have the level of prosperity you desire, money mastery is your key to prosperity. Here are some money mastery tips so prosperity can be yours:

You MUST spend more time focusing on abundance than you spend focusing on lack. Have you noticed how much time and energy you spend focusing on what you don't have instead of what you do have? It's easy to focus on the reality of "what is" rather than what you want. You can never look at lack and experience prosperity. I've heard clients *complain* if they receive a small monetary gift in the mail and focus on it *not being enough* money. Why not feel grateful despite it being a small amount of money? So many get caught up on what is *not* working that they are blind to what *is* working. It's important to celebrate even the small wins; big wins will soon follow.

Would you be upset if you won $1 million versus winning $300 million? If you won the lottery, would you focus on the amount of taxes you have to pay? Would you complain that people may only like you for your money? Worry they may try to steal your winnings? Do you talk yourself into being poor? I've seen many clients function in ungrateful states of mind, finding fault with everything around them and not taking the time to be *present* and *appreciative* of what they have versus what they don't have. A non-appreciative state is working against them in every aspect of their lives.

Do you dread paying bills or taxes? How about flipping that and *be grateful* you can pay these bills? If you were to visit a third world country, I guarantee you would be grateful for all your blessings. Many people in the world are living in extreme poverty and would give anything for the life you live. If you are worried about *"what is"* or how you're going to pay your bills, your money problems will only get worse. Every thought you *think* becomes part of the problem, or it can be the solution. Focus on the abundance flowing in your life and practice gratefulness.

Follow your bliss! Feelings of negativity, fear, shame, dread, worry, hatred or guilt will block abundance. Those are low-level emotional states. Desperate dissatisfaction will always keep you from what you want. In order to magnetize money into your life you must be in a higher state of emotional state such as joy, love, and gratitude.

Have you ever noticed that great things happen in your life whenever you have been in a joyful state of mind? Practice living in joy, do things you love and are passionate about, and choose to be around people that lift you up. Fill up your cup until it overflows! Many times when people go on vacation, things naturally fall into place because they are feeling good and in a joyful state.

You must be able to "receive" money. Can you *receive* money? Sounds simple, but you cannot receive abundance if you have a block to receiving. I've seen many of my clients that are afraid of having money and unknowingly push it away, yet complain they don't have it. You may feel like you *have* to work hard for money and won't accept it unless you did.

You must ask yourself if you're not good at receiving. Is prosperity scary to you, or do you feel unworthy? Is the responsibility of having money overwhelming, or do you feel guilty having abundance? If you can't *receive* money, how can money flow into your life?

You must "give" in order to receive abundance. Hoarding comes from a lackful mindset that you don't *trust* the universe is abundant, and that you have to hang onto everything you have, believing the world has limited resources. In order to open up abundance, you must give back in appreciation willingly and openly, and it will expand and return back to you. Give to a person, place, or organization that makes your heart sing—whether it's a church, charity you love, homeless person—it doesn't matter. Send the gift of love to the world and see it expand and return back to you tenfold. Giving must come from a happy place; it's never good to give out of guilt or when you are feeling negative emotions.

Get clear on your intentions. Many people say they want money but they don't have a clue what to do once they receive it. If you received $10 million tomorrow, what would you do with it? Is it scary to think about that? Are you excited about it, or do you feel confusion and overwhelm? If you are feeling any negative emotions in regards to this, it could be a block for you.

Not being clear on your intentions with money can mean you're neither serious nor ready for money to flow into your life. Have you noticed that you rarely get what you want when you are ambiguous? Decide *today* how much money you need to be financially free. Once you get clear and focused by stating specifically how much money you want and what you would do with it once you receive the money, only then will things fall into place, because it means you are prepared for it as if it already happened.

Money Mastery. You are the architect of your own reality. Your outer world reflects that of your inner world. Money *does not* control you, and if you think money is controlling you, then you're allowing it to. The more fearful you are of money, the more enslaved you are to it. Money will no longer control you once you realize money is *only* symbolic of your value, and your value can never be eradicated or controlled. *Your value is untouchable!* You were born with unique skills, talents, passion, and have intrinsic value to offer this world, which can never be taken from you. Money is only an *indication* of how you value yourself.

It's empowering to understand and ultimately master your money. I have seen many clients that dread looking at their money, so they avoid it. Avoiding it will make the problems worse. Any fear you have about money is in your mind and, just as in a relationship, you have to nurture it to make it thrive. Once you make the decision, you will realize that you were never a slave to money; you were the master all this time.

This is a financially based world, and money is an important tool for *living without limitations*. The more prosperous you are, the more you can serve others. Utilize your special talents, skills, and passion to your highest ability to help others. You cannot help many people when holding onto fear-based poverty conscious beliefs that no longer serve you.

There is much more to cover on this topic but here are some steps you must take to start shifting from poverty-based money slavery to prosperity-based money mastery.

RECAP:

1. **Release resistance.** Focus on abundance, and think thoughts that feel good. Acknowledge any lingering negative thoughts so they will dissipate, then shift your focus on abundance.

2. **Be in a blissful, joyful state as much as possible.** Do things you LOVE to do and fill up your cup with love, fun, and laughter.

3. **"Give and take."** *Give* to charities, people, or organizations you feel passionate about as a way of saying "thanks" for the blessings you have. Make sure you know how to *receive* money. The more you can receive, the more you can give.

4. **Get clear on your intentions.** Sit down and decide how much money you need to feel financially free. Make a list of things

you want to do with your abundance: donate to charity, what you would purchase, and how you will help and serve others.

5. **Realize you are deserving of money, and line up with abundance.** Master your relationship with money by learning what you need to know. This relationship must be well cared for it to thrive.

Follow these steps and not only will you have achieved **MONEY MASTERY** and find your **KEY TO PROSPERITY,** you will be well on your way to **LIVING WITHOUT LIMITATIONS!**

Stephen Yuzenko

Steve is the owner of Natural Success Coaching.

Married 28 years, he and his wife have three wonderful kids. He coaches and consults in areas of personal development, health & fitness, information technology, and businesses from single-person-startup to multi-million and multi-billion dollar corporations.

His passion is CONNECTION!

One of his mottos is "No matter what business you're in, it's a **people business.**" With degrees in Marketing, Business Administration, Accounting, and Computer Science, he has broadened his skills in the personal arena as a certified hypnotist.

His ENITRE FOCUS is on YOU and YOUR SUCCESS!

With Peace, Respect, & Love!

**Natural Success Coaching1323 W. Walnut Ave.
Ste 2-215Dalton, GA 30720**

www.NaturalSuccess.us

Skype: Steve.Yuzenko

✉ **info@naturalsuccess.us**

𝐟 **facebook.com/NaturalSuccessCoach**

🐦 **twitter.com/NaturalSuccess1**

CHAPTER 20

CRANKING IT UP! – LIVING YOUR LIFE OUT LOUD!

Stephen Yuzenko

Are you ready??? Let's CRANK IT UP!!!!

(Crank what up? What are you talking about?)

We are talking about CRANKING YOUR LIFE UP!

Life itself has many natural features. One inherent part of life is growth. Every living thing has this natural tendency. In this chapter I'm going to share some (secret?) knowledge with you. The funny thing about this "knowledge" is that somewhere, possibly deep inside of your thoughts, or even deeper…in your heart and soul, it exists. Maybe a better way of explaining what we're doing is that we're working together, so YOU can extract some POWERFUL knowledge, which will help you grow!

Take a moment to focus and listen… (Listen to what?) Listen to your heart! Let every other "noise" fade into the background. (Closing your eyes will help to limit distractions.) If you cup your hands over your ears, what do you hear; the ocean? (This is the sound of life! You hear the sounds that are resonating within and around you; the sounds of your environment/world and of your blood flowing through your body.) Ok, keep focusing… When I say "listen to your heart," it's not the sound of your heartbeat that you're listening for. (Then what am I listening for?) Listen to your true-heart—your soul. In your own quiet-space, listen to what your soul is longing for. Listen to what desires are within you. Listen to which one, or ones, are yearning to be heard…

However long this takes is ok. Be patient. It may take only a few seconds, or it may take several moments, minutes, or possibly many tries. The key is to focus your "listening" to identify what your soul desires.

Well, what if I don't hear anything? Then listen more… Listen deeper… You are a part of this vast universe, which (yes, audibly, as well as in many other ways that we have yet to even begin to understand) resonates to and through us. The key is to FOCUS, limit distractions, and then simply "listen"…

Once you "hear" this, it will begin a process. That natural-life process of growth will begin. This is EXCITING!!! You will start to feel the excitement! What does it feel like? Well, you know the feeling when you hear the first few notes of one of your all-time favorite songs? It's the feeling of wanting to listen, real close, and hoping that you've heard it right. Or maybe it's the first time you've heard your unborn baby's heartbeat? That's the feeling that makes you reach for the volume knob and CRANK IT UP!

Ok, now that I've listened and identified my desire, what do I do? How do I "CRANK IT UP?" First, congratulate yourself! Many people wait a long time, sometimes their whole lives, to "discover" what their heart and soul desire. You, my friend, have already cranked it up a notch above that!

While growth is a natural process, as we've said, so is our tendency to wait for things to come to us, manifest, or whatever… The ACTION that you took with focusing and listening is what MOVED YOU forward. So, let's keep using these natural forces (like Sir Isaac Newton's law… "An object at rest tends to stay at rest, and an object in motion tends to stay in motion.")! A thought, idea, and a soul-inspired mission are all things that we can control to create our desires.

Now that you have your desire in mind, and in motion, what's next? (Have you guessed?) Yes, let's CRANK IT UP!!! You've heard your soul's message. Some clients describe this in different ways, such as tapping into universal consciousness, listening to God, or simply getting in touch with your higher, or inner, self. Whatever YOU call "it," is what is important. What's even more important is your next ACTION to CRANK IT UP…which is to BELIEVE!

Believe that what you've heard from your soul is REAL, and that it is now part of your inherent natural process to make "it" happen! You know it is real, as you've heard and felt it already. As you take more actions to bring it to reality, it will grow stronger. You now know what you want, whether it is a mission to have, accomplish or become something; the seed has been planted. With the right actions, such as realizing and then further developing your belief, it will grow... naturally. Some may say it is like their "burning desire," or describe it in other terms.

For you to CRANK IT UP, you will need to feed-the-seed. (Similar to nourishing a plant to help it transform from a seed into a thriving bush or tree with the biggest, sweetest fruit you've ever tasted!) You can do this by visualizing it in as real terms as your mind and heart together can muster. See, smell, taste, feel, and hear it as it will BE, once your desire has been manifested. Do this as if you are watching a movie, seeing it happen, and then step into that movie. You will make some REAL progress by repeating this "visualization" exercise as often as you can. This process uses our unique gift of imagination.

At some point, you will notice "things" starting to happen. People with whom you need to connect will be there. Many times they will show up at just the right time, along with resources that do the same thing. Now, if you're thinking, all I have to do is "imagine," and all of my heart's desires will appear, then you are not quite there, yet. What you have to do to CRANK IT UP, is to keep your belief strong, practice your visualization and imagination, and then follow the next step...

What's the next step? Yep, you've got it right....CRANK IT UP! With this step, we're cranking up AWARENESS. Some of the world's greatest opportunities have passed right before people who were simply not aware. (It may have even happened to you?) Some clients have watched opportunities fly by, and once they realized it, they had to deal with one of the saddest emotions we, as humans, can experience—regret.

So what can I do to be more aware? To increase your awareness, start looking and "listening," just as you did to discover your desire. Tune into what you want. The pieces that you need to progress towards your goal may show up as a glimmer of light in a new idea, or even a slight whisper to turn in a slightly different direction. They may even show up in your mailbox! When you are aware, and hear that whisper, you already know what to do, right? CRANK IT UP!!! Make that call to the person who showed up in your awareness when visualizing, turn up that road when you are given the direction to go that way, and boldly reach out and grab that "opportunity" when it is presented to you!

PAY ATTENTION to the small things, as the smallest details in life can lead to the biggest rewards! (Attention = LOVE!) When you think about it, what you focus your attention towards, is what you love... Whether we're subconsciously focused, or using our full conscious attention, whatever receives our attention is what (or who) receives our love. The best part is that our focused attention is under our control in every moment. When you include focused awareness as a part of your focused attention, you are directing the movie of your life. Rather than letting outside factors (in whatever form they may be presented to you, such as someone's opinion, demands, events, or things that come into your life) control your direction, YOU CONTROL your course of direction! Paying CONSISTENT ATTENTION to the guidance that sparked, and drives, your heart's desire WILL LEAD YOU. It will lead you to the people and things that need to come into your life; TO SUCCESS!

Ok, are we at full volume yet? Are we movin' & groovin'? Swaying and jumping to the sound of our heart's song? What do you think? We're getting close...and we can still CRANK IT UP!

When you do everything in this chapter, you are growing and living. When you do them with LOVE, you are living your life out LOUD! Living out LOUD is the difference between a smirked-grin and an all-out belly laugh. You will begin, and then continue, to see positive and WONDERFUL things begin to happen in your life...

Let's review... Use life's natural tendency to grow. Focus, Listen (be patient), Take Action (getting started is a major step, and once started, momentum will be in your favor), Believe (in yourself, in your heart's desires, and know they are real), Heighten Your Awareness, Pay

Consistent Attention (especially to the small things that you once may have overlooked), and LOVE (start with yourself and let it spread to everyone and everything)!

Congratulations as you CRANK IT UP & Live Your Life Out Loud!

With RESPECT and LOVE.

Subira Folami

Rev Sensei Subira is a Minister, a Spiritual Life Coach, International Speaker and Social Media Marketing Trainer. She is founder and visionary of "Subira," a global movement called "Let Life Transform You" that highlights and celebrates the power of the human spirit to triumph over seeming adversity by being a willing and deliberate participant with life. Subira supports and inspires empathy-driven leaders, visionaries, and entrepreneurs on their personal path to remembering wholeness, by spreading the message of what is possible when you develop an intimate understanding of consciously connecting to and using the power of Universal Principles coupled with hope and healing to move elegantly through life's transformations.

"Rev Sensei" as Subira is affectionately called, has studied Martial Arts since 1989. She holds a first degree black belt in American Kenpo and a yellow belt in Aikido. In addition, she has integrated the training of Budokon, which is a fusion of yoga, martial arts and lifestyle training.

www.workwithsubira.com

f facebook.com/alicia.r.hillFB

f facebook.com/workwithsubira

▶ youtube.com/PathOfSacredWarrior

𝕏 twitter.com/workwithsubira

in linkedin.com/pub/alicia-r-hill/10/703/846

CHAPTER 21

THE LAW OF APPRECIATION: THE SACRED WHISPERING OF YOUR HEART

Subira Folami

You're a good person, considerate of puppies, babies and kind to your fellow man, so you don't understand why you find yourself in this painful situation. Sometimes it has been so painful that it feels like your entire Life is being uprooted from your core; your heart may be breaking such that you feel like you are dying. Well, guess what? Parts of you are dying. Transformation is a process in which parts of you (outdated thoughts, stagnant relationships, work that no longer fulfills you) will submit to the new, the higher vibrational energy that is seeking an outlet through you. Simply put, you are being called to a higher expression of yourself, and that calling can be disconcerting to say the least.

Today you find yourself crying out to the "Powers That Be," asking, no, pleading to understand why this is happening *to you*, and you may even be asking why God would allow this to happen *to you*. Life is about forward movement and expansion. Life is always seeking out new people who will allow It to experience an expanded expression of Itself. During these times, my clients have come to recognize that Life continually offers us the opportunity to heal. And healing only takes place when you consciously apply love and appreciation to those places, situations and people where you find resistance and pain. The Universe is so gracious and mindful that the first person to benefit from the love and appreciation that you will apply to the resistance and pain is Y-O-U.

Think about it, if you've ever taken any form of exercise; be it yoga, martial arts or weight lifting, you are quite literally stretching yourself on a physical level; and after each session, you can lift a few more pounds or you find that you have become more flexible and strong.

Somewhere in your process, you also find that you actually have an appreciation for yourself and the work you have done, as well as for your personal trainer and the entire experience. This is so even though while you were in the thick of it, muscles throbbing, sweat pouring profusely from your face, you may have had more than a few choice words for the experience, your personal trainer and even for yourself for choosing to transform this part of your life.

It is in this place within yourself that you can hear the sacred whispering of appreciation that your heart is sending throughout your body. The process of transformation is cleansing and recalibrating your nervous system and your psyche, so that the Universal Law of Appreciation can begin Its work of attracting to you all that you require. This way, when you get to the other side of the transformation, you will be an entirely new Being who engages with the world in a whole new way; with a heart full of love and joy and appreciation.

As a Spiritual Life Coach, I want to offer you some new, more empowering ways to understand what is happening *through you* as well as some tools to support you in navigating your transformative journey. Maybe you are at the beginning and just recently getting that intuitive nudge that something is underfoot; or perhaps you are in the thick of the transformation where often we find ourselves rendered unable to hear or see clearly. Or perhaps you are at the end of this particular transformation, and at least for the time being, you have made it to the other side. Regardless where you find yourself right now, I offer that from this point forward, you orient yourself from the inside rather than attempting to understand what is happening with your mind, eyes and ears.

Seven Level Healing Paradigm~Universal Principles are tools to help you transform:

Know Yourself: You will come to KNOW YOURSELF by being willing to become awake to who you really are, to acknowledge and accept all parts of yourself.

See Yourself: Take quiet time with yourself. Allow yourself the time and space to have reflective time, so that you can explore your heart and begin to SEE YOURSELF in a more expansive way.

Accept Yourself: You will be able to ACCEPT your human complexities and inconsistencies, if you can understand that those frailties are your way of reaching out for love.

Be Yourself: This is the place where you will find true freedom. Once you have awakened, gained an awareness and are able to accept yourself for who you authentically are, it is easy to BE YOURSELF.

Honor Yourself: At this place on your transformational journey, you no longer discount, deny or gloss over who you are, what your intuition is telling you, or what you feel in HONORING YOURSELF. You get comfortable engaging with the deluge of power that you are able to flow, because the obstructions are being healed away.

Trust Yourself: When you connect with yourself as an essential aspect of Spirit, when you begin to understand that your core is being cleaned up and exposed in this transformative process, you will feel safe again; because you know that the Universal Intelligence flows through you, informing you with each new step. You can now TRUST YOURSELF.

Appreciate Yourself: This last step in the healing process is a gift from Spirit specifically for you: Its BeLoved child in whom It is well pleased. You will be lavishly provided for by Spirit. You will be taught by Spirit how to demonstrate to yourself that you do indeed love yourself, and that you are worthy of your own time and attention. You no longer wait around for someone outside yourself to APPRECIATE YOU, because you now love loving yourself.

Below are a few new paradigms that will support you in moving forward:

Every relationship you are a part of is experiencing transformation with you. All of them. Some will get stronger, others will come to completion, and new people will be introduced into your world. The people you hope will handle this well might not be able to for a variety of reasons. Forgive yourself and them quickly, as everyone is doing their absolute best, and because no one plans for major life transformations. Carrying bitterness, resentment or anger won't help you move forward. Fighting for anyone to stick with you won't console you. Those who can, will. Appreciate those who stay and those who chose to go because both have added something extraordinary to your life even if you can't see it or feel it right now.

You are going to need all of your energy to transform. You will convince yourself that you are thinking straight, are able to handle all of this and do not need anyone. You will run out of fuel. Amazingly, the body accepts that things have changed before the mind. After a life-altering transformation, your sense of self will never be the same. Embrace this. Your old self was great. Your transformed self will be even better. Surrender to what is happening, and you will learn to trust that wherever LIFE is taking you is amazing beyond your most creative imaginings.

You are bigger than the fear and the pain. Even if you are normally stubborn, confident and seemingly invincible, you will finally find yourself admitting that you feel afraid—especially if physical or psychological pain is a part of your transformative process. The unknown will eat at you. You will feel normal eventually; the thing is that it will be a new kind of normal. When you feel afraid let yourself lean on those around you. Cry. Allow yourself to be vulnerable. There will be time for strength but for now, let it all out. Yell if you need to. Sing when you feel up to it. Sob uncontrollably and never apologize for feeling your emotions. Not giving yourself over to this experience fully will leave you stuck; and remember LIFE is about moving forward and expansion.

The people that love you are just as frightened as you are. Probably more. They will be worrying even when they are smiling. They will assume you are in more pain than you are. They will go through a process that you will never understand, just like they will never understand the process you are going through. Let them process. Forgive them when they don't understand. Exercise patience when you can. Know that those that were built for this will be there when you get to the other side, and you will all be able to laugh together again. You'll cry together too. Then you'll get to a place where you will just live in the world again together.

When you get to the other side you'll be amazed. You're going to feel like the future is a funny thing to think about, because the present is going to suddenly seem incredibly important. Keep moving forward.

Meet new people that connect to the newly evolved version of your old self. Let go of those that don't "get" who you are now, and do your best not to feel guilty about letting go; it's just time. The greatest gift you've been given is that you now have a deep understanding that you're going to make the most of every second. Be the most passionate person you know going forward. Translate that passion to a higher purpose that is underscored by the knowing that this transformation process has tuned you in to the sacred whispering of your heart, and you now exude appreciation for it all.

Donna Apilado-Schumacher

Donna Apilado-Schumacher is a small business startup coach, consultant, QuickBooks trainer, and entrepreneur.

She has been a force in the small business world for over 25 years, leading improvements in operations, human resources, management, sales, purchasing, administration and accounting.

Apilado-Schumacher started AkamaiBooks, LLC a small business solutions provider and bookkeeping firm founded in Hawaii in 2006. She is passionate about transforming the economics of this country one small business startup at a time. She loves coaching and consulting with entrepreneurs and budding entrepreneurs to start the ideal small business and manage it in the most efficient way possible.

www.akamaibooks.com

plus.google.com/u/0/b/100896246496326836442/ 100896246496326836442/posts

✉ **donna@akamaibooks.com**

❶ **facebook.com/AkamaiBooks**

🐦 **twitter.com/akamaibooks**

🔗 **linkedin.com/pub/donna-apilado-schumacher/22/900/474**

CHAPTER 22

BLEND CLARITY AND FOCUS FOR A MORE EFFECTIVE AND PEACEFUL YOU

Donna Apilado-Schumacher

The alarm clock goes off at 5:00 a.m. Bleary-eyed, Jane slowly makes her way into the kitchen and pours herself a cup of coffee. "Thank goodness for the automatic timer on the coffee maker," she thinks to herself. In her half-awake state she skims through the morning paper, she checks her emails, all the while in the background the morning news updates her on world events. She glances at the clock, she glances at her schedule for the day; she calculates if she's running on schedule. She's got a half hour to squeeze in a workout and then another half hour to make the kids' breakfast and pack their lunches, and another half hour to shower and get ready for the day. It's going to be another marathon just getting out the door. She glances at all her tasks for the day and the week; she wonders how she's going to pack it all in—work, clients, school, kids, kids' afterschool and weekend activities, family time, social gatherings, grocery shopping, dinner, homework, honey-time, me time (what's that?)… The list seems endless, she's feeling drained from just thinking about it all and the week has only just begun.

As a small business consultant and small business startup coach, I have heard the above story so many times, as well as the following: "I am feeling overwhelmed!" or "Why am I even doing all of this?" "I don't even know where to begin!" "I love my family, but I just can't breathe!" "How can I think of even starting a new business when I don't even have time to do all that's in my life as it is!"

With a more than full life, it can feel overwhelming and chaotic. That's why I love working with individuals to help them find that clarity and prioritize their life according to their dreams—which often include starting their own small business. Many clients, friends, and people I meet feel overburdened by the myriad of interests, responsibilities, and commitments in their everyday life. And with technology, life has become even more complicated and faster than ever!

I've seen people give up, or "temporarily" put their personal and business dreams on hold, just so they can tackle all the rest of the responsibilities in their lives, only to find themselves unhappy and somewhat resentful. Other people pursue other people's dreams (parents, partners, employers, spouse, and friends) and not their own. Others drown themselves in mind-numbing substances to deny the existence of their own personal dreams. Still others go on buying sprees trying to fill that void that never seems to be filled.

My question to you is, "What's standing in the way of you pursuing your dreams?"

Clarity

Clarity can be brought forth through the daily practice of emptying your mind. It is only when you make this time to empty your mind that you will create space for clarity to move forth within.

Many clients like to empty their minds either by taking a walk on the beach, having a hot bubble bath, or going for a run. This is a wonderful way to increase one's performance and productivity as well as clear decision-making in the everyday business/work world.

A quick and easy morning technique appears toward the end of this chapter. Use it for those busy days when you only have five to ten minutes to squeeze in to your morning.

NOW, what does clarity look and feel like to you?

I encourage you to make a list of all the things that you like to do to clear your mind and schedule them into each day.

Getting to Know and Focusing on Your "True North"

What emotional states do you value most in your life? Is it joy, adventure, success, or is it just feeling healthy and vibrant?

How, and by what means or goals, do you achieve these emotional states? For some clients, it may mean spending time with the family that brings them great joy and happiness. Some want to be more carefree, and like parachuting out of an airplane. Many enjoy working out their bodies to feel healthy and vibrant. Others start their own small business with the dream of someday making millions!

These emotional states and their corresponding means and goals are your compass – your "true north." Your desired emotional states drive you to create goals that lead to projects that lead to tasks.

What emotional states do you value most? Prioritize them. Then, take your list of projects and tasks, and ask yourself the question on each, "How does this relate to my values and goals? Is it serving at least one or several of my life's values and goals?" Prioritize your projects and tasks according to your prioritized set of values and goals and start eliminating those that do not serve your values and goals.

Peace

How do we regain peace? By aligning the myriad of tasks in our everyday lives with our "true north," as well as taking the time to empty our minds. Oftentimes one can be surrounded by a peaceful setting and still not feel at peace. This is because our thoughts are not at peace. Our thoughts are in control, in the driver's seat, controlling our emotional state and keeping us from feeling peace.

A clear mind brings forth clarity, which then helps us to choose wisely, aligning ourselves even closer to our "true north" which then, brings us to further peace.

SIMPLE MORNING EXERCISE

Turn on some calm meditation music.

Get into a relaxed comfortable position, close your eyes, relax your body, and let go.

Take Several Cleansing Breaths.... Exhale and let it all out several times.

While taking these breaths know that you are being supported by a source greater than you. Know this and have confidence that this is true.

Five to Ten Minutes to Clear Your Mind

Focus on your breath... in.... and out... in... and out.... Thoughts will come; let them float by, do not attach yourself to any thought, let each one go. Bring your mind back to your breath. Again, thoughts will come, let them go by, and keep bringing your mind back to your breath. Let your thoughts pass, don't hold on to a thought, watch all thoughts go by. Do this for five to ten minutes daily.

Say an Affirmation to End the Exercise and Begin the Day

Find, customize or create affirmations for your various emotional and spiritual needs. Words are powerful, so make sure the words you use really work for you and truly move you. Pick an affirmation that is appropriate for whatever area you feel you need for that day. Say the affirmation several times out loud until the words have sunken in to your core. Begin your day with confidence and clarity.

POINTS TO REMEMBER

Evolution of YOU leads to more stuff to do – it's a good thing!

Know and accept that YOU are an evolving being, filled with the desire to create! This desire for creating leads to many thoughts and ideas, which then lead to the myriad of projects and tasks that eventually become things. The point here is, there will always be a sense of pressure within you driven by your dreams, by your desires to create. There is, and always will be stuff to do! Embrace this fact into your life and relax into it.

Alignment is Key

All too often in life, we end up focusing on the distractions that don't relate to or serve our values and goals. The major question to ask with all of your projects and tasks is, "How is this serving my life's values and goals?" Does what you are doing ultimately point back toward your set of values in life? Are they in alignment? It is these distractions we choose that do not align that keep us from attaining all that we want in life. Choose wisely.

It's the Journey, not the End

Enjoy and be fueled by the journey and do NOT hold on to tunnel vision with only the end in mind as your major focus. We were raised to think that happiness and peace will come when... Even the messages we receive in society tell us that we must get this, or do that and THEN we will be happy. Don't wait to be happy, just choose to be happy NOW. What you are wanting will come; however, it is the journey that builds your magnificence.

Go For It!

Imagine it is near the end of your life, the end of your journey on this plane of existence. As you look back upon your life, will it be with a sense of peace knowing you gave it your ALL? Stay the course of your "true north," enjoy the journey and GO FOR IT! You WILL arrive at your destinations with clarity and peace.

Teresa Mason Maron

Teresa Mason Maron was a former National Champion Ballroom competitor when she developed a passion for Energy Medicine.

She was amazed at how effective it was for manifesting positive outcomes, maintaining physical strength, and managing stress.

She began by using breath, visualization and intention techniques, combined with the energy of movement. This brought her new understanding of the energy field.

Teresa now shares her passion with the world through online classes, a weekly radio show, speaking engagements and her private practice.

Teresa is currently developing a documentary film about Holistic treatments for Alzheimer's sufferers, called Dance to Remember.

www.JoyfulJourneys.us

CHAPTER 23

THE TRUE VALUE OF STRESS; FROM OVERWHELMED TO OVERJOYED

Teresa Mason Maron

As your Holistic practitioner, I am concerned about the effects of stress on our bodies and our lives. I want to share with you a new approach.

Through working with hundreds of people, I have noticed something that we all have in common.

Our Only Enemy is Stress.

Energy Medicine combines ancient techniques with the cutting edge possibilities of technology. I find this the most exciting health and wellness development of our time, as traditional Medicine and Holistic techniques go hand in hand to create opportunities for each of us to take more control of how we feel.

The Chakras are 7 energy centers that are located up and down your spine, both sending and receiving energy. The Base and the Crown Chakras are vertical, sending energy down into the ground, and up, through the top of your head. The other 5 Chakras are horizontal, sending energy both in front and behind you. Think of this as being surrounded in a circle of Vibrating energy. Each Chakra sends out a signal, your personal vibration, and anchors a Spiritual purpose, just for you. The body responds with a physical symptom if the Spiritual purpose is being ignored, and your signal will weaken.

Example: a blocked Base Chakra will cause you to lose confidence, and wonder about your life purpose.

- Base Chakra—Red—Creates Strength and Vitality, Life Force, and Finding Your Life's Purpose
- Sacral Chakra—Orange—Healthy Boundaries, Experiencing Joy, and Feeling Safe
- Solar Plexus Chakra—Yellow—Adrenals, Digestion, Responding, Not Reacting
- Heart Chakra—Green—Heart, Lungs, Blood Pressure, Compassion, Empathy and Unconditional Love
- Throat Chakra—Blue—Thyroid, Metabolism, Communication Sensitivity, Personal Truth
- Third Eye Chakra—Indigo—Eyes, Nose Ears, Pituitary
- Trust Others, Intuition, Know Yourself, Discernment
- Crown Chakra—Violet—Brain, nervous system, Pineal Feeling connected, and harmonious Desire to Serve

Your energy field expands and contracts as needed. In quiet time alone, you will automatically pull in your field. Entering a crowded room, you will expand, and when talking or communicating, your field will mix with another's field.

Being conscious of this adds power to the process, and setting intention on your communications with others is highly effective.

Chakras are affected by relationships, situations, events and especially your emotional reactions.

Stress from exposure to toxins, bad diet, conflict, deadlines and electronic devices, all add to an energetic build up that might be seen as a cloud or a blockage, also called an imprint. This weakens your signal.

Accidents, traffic, surgery, grief, fear and anger cause the opposite problem, a rip or a tear in your field. This wastes your signal.

The blockage causes you to shut down, like you can't breathe, and the rips cause a nervous feeling, because you are losing energy like a poorly insulated house in winter.

You are said to be "Balanced" when all chakra centers are at neither of these extremes, working together to keep you healthy. This is the first step in Energy Balance.

Listen to what your body is telling you, because stress affects us first in our Energy field.

The cause of all disease is stress.

The Value of Stress is that when you become more aware of the damage that stress causes, and take steps to reverse that damage sooner, you stay in preventative care, instead of allowing stress to get you into crisis management care. This is very self-empowering, healing symptoms of stress before they enter your physical body.

What you are thinking, feeling and saying is affecting you, and everyone around you.

Our bodies regenerate new cells about every 21 days. As we become more positive, remove more stress from our lives and feel more Joy, we create better cells. We can reverse the signs of aging and heal disease by creating better cells faster than we create substandard ones. Being aware of our chakra system, and what part of the body each represents, keeps you conscious of the process of creating better cells. What could be a better way to live?

What you think is what you create, and how you feel is the barometer of how well you are doing it!

The way you feel when everything clicks, and when your life is being created in the moment, with intent and purposeful living, is the feeling of being energetically balanced.

Balance is experienced as a constantly shifting and very alive dynamic, like a beautiful dance. The chakra activity is both adding and removing energy from your centers based on need, expressed by your thoughts, words and emotions. We have all felt this way at one time or another, but stress is the enemy. When we are balanced, problem solving, gut instincts and feeling good is easy, and so being balanced means we remain healthy on all levels, creating beautiful cells.

How Chakra Energy gets unbalanced is pretty simple. When you have gone to the well one too many times to pull off the "I have to make this work" syndrome, and you feel like you are running on fumes, without proper rest, exercise and food, and are unable to balance your life in the form of time, or commitments, and you are not putting yourself on the to do list, you are overly stressed. Being too accessible by cell phone, having no patience with yourself and scheduling your days too tightly can eventually wear down the natural Chakra function of Energetic Balance.

Stress is said to be subconscious when you are in denial, and are consciously giving yourself the pep talk. Everything is fine!

Or, it can come from past disappointments and sorrows that you are burying in a deep memory. Don't go there!

If, through subconscious stress, you become unable to create balance naturally, you will feel blocked, or overwhelmed, and it becomes complicated as more imprints occur.

When one becomes blocked or over stimulated, this is the progression of how stress is working into your chakra centers.

- First, emotions get out of control, creating drama all around you. Big events seem meaningless, and little things set you off. This is a great time to make some changes.

- Then thought processes get confused, and a lack of discernment, bad decisions and irrational behavior are common. Oops, don't make decisions now.

- Finally physical symptoms occur, and the part of the body affected is very telling of the source of the problem. Don't medicate, meditate.

This also serves as an explanation of why it is so important to have nothing but positive thoughts. As you think the thoughts, they are being created right into your reality as your physical body. Figures of speech are uncanny in the creation process. Be very careful with the choices.

Examples:

- That just burns me up.
- I just shot myself in the foot.
- When I heard that it almost gave me a heart attack!
- Don't shoot the messenger!
- Stop, that is so funny it's killing me!

The flip side of that is if you are mindful of your thoughts and words you can create whatever you want. So what do you want? Let me help you make that all important list. First, look at this chart to answer the question:

ARE YOUR CHAKRAS BALANCED?

Symptoms of Balance

1. Base—Optimistic, Curious, Assertive, Loves Humor
2. Sacral—Creative, Colorful, Adventurous
3. Solar Plexus—Clarity, Easy Going, Organized
4. Heart—Positive self-image, compassion, service
5. Throat—Great communicator, comfortable, truth
6. Third Eye—Sensitive to Others, Observant, Soothing
7. Crown—Connected on every level, Peace, Justice

Symptoms of Unbalanced

1. Base—Apathetic, Sleepy, Unmotivated
2. Sacral—Upset, Non Productive, Nervous
3. Solar Plexus—Stomach Pain, fear, doubts
4. Heart—Separation anxiety, rejection, depression
5. Throat—Sarcasm, trouble sleeping, laryngitis
6. Third Eye—Headaches, Bad Memory, Loss of Focus
7. Crown—Loner, disciplined with low threshold of joy

If you find yourself frequently saying, "I'm too busy," as an excuse for not doing something that you would enjoy, then maybe you are too busy. What can you do about that? Slow down, of course, be kind to yourself and set boundaries that first and foremost honor your health.

Because when your chakras have been overworked to balance such ruinous activity to the point when they can no longer repair the damage, this stress will enter the physical body as disease, and with increasing frequency, and severity.

The cure is simple. Every time you feel stress, make a conscious decision to explore the feeling purposefully. Find the true cause of the stress, and look at options to reduce or eliminate that set of circumstances from your life.

First of all, what a shift in the way you handle it. Instead of stress owning you, just think, "Excellent! I feel stress! Perfect, because now I get to eliminate another subconscious trigger. What is really at the root of this stressful moment?"

When you start to prioritize differently, and put anything that causes stress under the microscope, your life will start to change. You will realize that anything you have to "make work" is no longer right for you. This is the true value of stress.

Jan Robberts

Having been an avid student of personal development for many years, Jan came to realize that a positive attitude is an enormous asset in all walks of life. Always hungry for more and wanting to fulfil his burning passion for helping others, he enrolled into several years of training in the Coaching Cognition Academy and started to coach.

Afterwards, Jan also became a certified Coach, Trainer and Speaker with the John Maxwell Team, where he is continually getting better equipped in the Mentorship Program. He began to realize another passion as well: working with youth; By intentionally listening to them he felt a desperate need for support and understanding with an alarmingly increasing challenge in our schools, clubs and on the internet; Bullying!

By listening to parents he also discovered their anguish of not knowing how to find out, and what to do about this delicate situation. Stories are unfolding and coaching has become even more satisfying.

www.johncmaxwellgroup.com/janrobberts/

Skype: robberts7487

✉ jan.robberts@yahoo.co.uk

f facebook.com/jan.robberts

𝕏 twitter.com/Robberts

in no.linkedin.com/pub/jan-robberts/22/167/878/

CHAPTER 24

BREAKING THROUGH THE BONDAGE OF BULLYING

Jan Robberts

Bullying is something that has been going on for many years in schools, clubs, our neighborhoods, our work...both Physically and Mentally.

Most of the time it is difficult to detect, as kids are very clever at hiding it from their friends, their brothers and sisters, their parents and teachers, for a variety of reasons.

Fear of retribution, lack of trust, embarrassment, acceptance because they feel unworthy, difficulties within the families, "nobody will believe me,"...the list goes on...

How then will a parent ever be able to help and support their children through this terrible ordeal, which can have devastating consequences to a point where a child will end it all by taking his or her own life?

Social media and all the modern appliances used to "communicate," such as tablets and media phones, bring yet another dimension to this huge challenge as now Cyber Bullying is growing rapidly in the one and only sanctuary our children still had....their bedrooms.

Parents tell me in our Coaching sessions they sometimes notice a change in their children, but are concerned if it is just puberty and all that goes with it, different friends, music, video games... Some of my clients have expressed concerns about if they worry too much. Are they over protective and should they give their kids some space, a chance to grow up rather than interfere in everything they do?

Many of my clients find it difficult to discover what, if anything, is wrong with their children, because sometimes they can be "moody creatures," not wanting to listen to "The Voice of Authority"...and what do parents know anyway...those relics of the past who just wouldn't understand.

So what then can parents do to find out what is going on in their child's life without giving them the wrong impression? (Caring is never wrong, though.)

How can we help you as a parent or guardian to discover if you are sure this *is* really happening,... your precious child is really getting bullied, so you can take action and support your child to get through this painful ordeal, even get external help if necessary? (And/or available?)

As a Coach I have asked parents what they have noticed to be different about their child. "There must have been *something* for you to be questioning yourself and seek help..."

"Have you noticed your child seems lethargic and does not want to get up in the mornings when he or she used to be very punctual and bright as a button before?"

"What have you noticed about their dress sense lately? What would you say about their taste in music? The kids they hang about with? Their attitude and interests? How are they performing in school? What can you tell me about their after school activities? How do you feel about any answers they give to anything you ask? "

Basically, what if anything, has changed about their habits? The list of questions could go on but it all depends on the answers you supply and the answers you are looking for...

Clients tell me that sometimes this problem gets exacerbated by being stressed themselves, trying to make ends meet; and some of the parents were themselves bullied in the past or are getting bullied at work by colleagues or a very persistent boss.

We do have to ask ourselves if at times we aren't guilty of some form of bullying with our very own kids without meaning to or even realizing it, by calling them names, negative remarks about their hairstyles or clothes...even if it's "just for fun!"...We must always remember that these children, *our* children could be just one word away from their breaking point and committing suicide. Would you want to have that on your conscience? Were you the last one to talk to them, and what did you say?

Hindsight is a great thing...or is it?

You hear about it in the news, on the television, from other parents.... and I hear that more and more now but, until it happens to *your* child, until it stares *you* in the face...

Since I started coaching parents about bullying I began looking for more information, and I'm discovering some horrifying facts about the percentage of kids getting bullied, about the percentage of our youth committing suicide... it would surprise and shock you how often this happens...increasing daily with cyber bullying.

My heart aches every time I hear about another case. A whole life ahead of them, and they cannot see themselves with a future, they no longer want to live, because the present hurts so bad. How could it *ever* get any better...

Our kids need to know we care, that we love them unconditionally, that we are there for them if they ever see the need to talk, that we won't judge them...however hard that might sometimes be...

I recommend praising our children for what they are doing right, regardless of what mistakes they make. I am not talking of discipline when they have made some bad choices which will have consequences; but even then we must seek for reasons, seek to understand...

We have to encourage our kids, empower them, make them feel safe at home and affirm that whatever bothers them just now, the future looks much better....

Oh, affirmations;

There are many ways to affirm both as parents and our children and I am sure you could think of some great affirmations to put together and repeat many times a day but I can give you some ideas to get started:

"Today is the first day of the rest of my beautiful life."

"I deserve the very best, as I am a unique and wonderful child, with goals and dreams which I will achieve by working towards them every day."

"Every day I am thankful and grateful for waking up and getting another chance to be the best I can be."

"I am an amazing parent, and the love for my children is pure and has no limits."

"I appreciate my class mates, and my strength will protect them, not hurt them."

"Today I will no longer call my friends names which make them feel bad, but I will lift them up to make them feel better."

"My positive attitude is so contagious, even my enemies become my friends."

"I am a perfect role model for my children, and they see me as their hero."

The list could go on and on…and includes affirmations for parents, victims and bullies.

At first I was amazed but when people got to know I had started to coach parents about bullying, they started to come forward, wanting help with their suspicion that their child *is* the bully as well.

It is always easy to forget the plight of those who do the bullying, as we can only see the damage they are doing. But we must not forget to do whatever we can to help them too, as most of the time, there are reasons they do what they do.

They often hide their own insecurities, their own hurts, their own misfortunes and abuse behind a mask of bravado of masculinity, of "girl power," a lack of recognition, of having been bullied themselves.

(This includes boys and girls, sisters and brothers, parents, teachers, bosses and colleagues...)

When did you notice a change? What made you think this could be more serious than you thought?

What do you think you can do to be a positive influence in their lives?

How do you feel as a parent? How would you like your relationship with your children to improve?

It is so easy to see yourself as a failure, but you must remember, you are a tremendous parent and a great example to your children.

So many questions, from parents of both sides, so few answers...and the bullying goes on and on.

We all have a responsibility as parents, as teachers, as leaders and, NO, it is not OK to let this go on because you don't know how to handle it...to turn a blind eye in school hoping it will pass. We must all look into this much more closely, to connect more as a family, as a community and to let our children know it's not ever OK and encourage them to stand up and speak up...to be a relief to other kids, to be their hero, their role model...God knows, we can always do with more role models.

Listening to my clients, there is a drastic need for support on a local level, where kids can get help, where they can go when they don't directly want to talk to their parents....

A typical question I get asked often is, "How *do* you handle a situation like this?"

Our children are our future. We are always busy to save our planet with reductions of harmful gases, protecting endangered species...

We must realize that, without our help, our support and our love, our youth will grow up to be that endangered dysfunctional species.

We cannot, and must not let this happen; our kids deserve better. Let's give them Hope, and help them to live a life without limitations.

Warren Broad

Warren Broad is a clinical Hypnotherapist, life coach, and addictions specialist. Also a retired fireman. Warren began his counseling career, as a group home worker. Working with displaced youth and foster children, Warren quickly learned that coaching and counseling was his life's calling. Warren's education is extensive, holding multiple diplomas in adult psychology, clinical hypnosis, an honors diploma in addictions counseling, and certified coach. Warren continues to add to his education annually.

Warren lives 2 hours north of Toronto, Ontario in Canada with his wife, son, and 3 rescued dogs. From there Warren runs his in-person and online coaching and counseling practice. Warren is also often found on the tennis court, and volunteering in many local organizations. Warren's passion for helping individuals through their challenges is endless.

www.warrenrbroad.com

✉ **hello@warrenrbroad.com**

f **facebook.com/pages/Online-Counsellorca**

CHAPTER 25

SHIFT OUT OF YOUR SELF-DESTRUCTIVE CYCLE

Warren Broad

As a coach, hypnotherapist, and addictions specialist I have been working with addictions and compulsive behaviors for almost ten years. I have personally broken the addiction cycle, and I love to see when my clients succeed and take their lives back. Working with a coach lets you feel empowered that you are not alone and that there is someone that "has your back." It is my greatest pleasure to walk hand in hand with individuals as they break free of their old limiting beliefs and behaviors.

The following are scenarios and common themes within the world of addictions and compulsions. If any of these stories resonate with you please reach out to myself or a local coach that can help you break the bonds of addiction or compulsions. You are not alone.

David is a successful tradesman with more than 30 years' experience in his field. Once married with two children, his life began to unravel when his younger daughter developed multiple sclerosis. The stress magnified existing difficulties in his marriage, which ended shortly after his daughter passed away.

David started gambling as a way to take his mind off the stresses awaiting him at home. He needed that break between work and home and enjoyed the rush of playing the slots.

That welcome break soon became a craving, and the half hour ended up being two. Once a week, turned into nearly every day. Twenty dollars soon became several hundred, and before he knew it, his paycheck was spent by Monday, and he had no money to buy food.

Janice grew up in an environment marked by high expectations and low acceptance. Nothing she did was ever good enough to please her parents. Dreading going home, she spent as much time as possible with "friends," who introduced her to alcohol and recreational drugs at a young age.

These habits followed Janice out of the country and into the city, when she left right after high school. She was working, and was able to afford more alcohol and stronger drugs. Her first marriage, best characterized by co-dependence and heavy substance abuse, quickly ended and led to a second one with someone just as unsuitable but for different reasons. That too soon broke up. More alcohol and drugs were consumed simultaneously as a release and a punishment, because Janice blamed herself for what her life had become but needed to escape from what her life had evolved into.

From the outside, Maria had a good life growing up. Her parents had good jobs and were active in their community. They regularly attended a church where they volunteered wherever needed.

Home was another story. Her parents did not spend time with her and never told her they loved her. If she ever got into trouble, which was rare, they jumped all over her, but when that subsided they resumed leaving her alone. Never having been told she mattered, Maria turned to food and sex for comfort. Her low self-esteem led to several relationships characterized by abuse and neglect.

Each of these stories is characterized by someone in pain. David watched his daughter die before his eyes, powerless to do anything about it. Then he saw his wife leave him when he most needed her. Janice was never properly accepted at home, by those whose acceptance plays the most crucial role in any person's healthy development. Forced to find it elsewhere, she held on to the first people who gave her attention, even though that attention was not healthy but highly damaging. Maria also needed love and for someone to tell her she was fine the way she was.

These situations also highlight our need for relationship, and the important roles people play in our lives. When in pain, we need healthy relationships the most, but if they are not present, we can encounter trouble. David wanted to turn to his wife, but she chose to leave. Both Janice and Maria could not turn to their parents, so they sought out other relationships, and when those did not suffice they turned to or increased their use of unhealthy substances.

Pain is a part of life. We will all experience it at different points. When we do, we need to seek out positive and constructive human relationships. By contacting a qualified therapist, you begin to look at your life from a different viewpoint, getting feedback and help from someone whose only goal is to help you make your life better.

The first thing a coach will do is actually listen to you, and help you create a new vision for your life.

A coach will not judge you. You are valued from the moment you walk in the door.

Many people benefit from the simple act of sharing their pain for possibly the first time ever. The emotional release makes them feel as if a heavy burden has been taken off their shoulders. Something that feels and looks one way inside can take on a different appearance once spoken aloud.

The coach sees what works and what does not. The coach helps guide you to clarity and realization of your dreams, and the life you want to live.

David, Janice and Maria all benefited greatly from hearing someone say, "Your pain is legitimate. It's normal to feel that way in your situation." They accepted their pain, as opposed to not feeling accepted, which only adds to that pain.

The solutions can be as unique as the person. Coaching does not need to follow any pre-scripted process. David participated in a program with his coach where he learned about what caused his addiction to gambling. David also shares his struggles and frustrations with other men in a safe group environment.

For Janice, the healing began when a co-worker told her she was not fooling anybody. This came as a shock, as Janice considered herself highly functioning and able to keep her problems away from the workplace. A friend gave her the name of a coach that worked for her. With her coach, she began to see the errors in her thinking, and began to develop new ways to manage and visualize her life.

With the help of her coach, Maria realized for the first time the significant negative role food played in her life. Having learned the feelings that trigger her emotional eating, Maria now recognizes them. Instead of eating, she chooses one of many healthy activities she substitutes for the ice cream, such as going for a walk or calling a friend.

David, Janice and Maria did not wake up one day and say that was the day they would get addicted to their vice. It happened slowly, without them even knowing what was actually happening. At the heart of all three situations were hurt and low self-worth.

Through meeting and helping hundreds of people like David, Janice and Maria, coaches are able to help you avoid unnecessary pain and anguish which can lead to mistakes that can last a lifetime.

If you answer yes to any of the following questions, you will benefit from visiting a coach:

- When you encounter stress, is your first thought to drink alcohol, use sex, take drugs, eat or gamble? Is that how you "blow off steam?"
- Do you wish you had more friends?
- Do you feel that when you take drugs, drink, or act out you "loosen up" and become a more interesting person?
- Do you find yourself thinking about gambling, sex, drugs or alcohol when you are not around them?
- Have you noticed changes in your most important relationships? Are people avoiding you?
- Are you missing increased amount of time from work and other activities because of your behaviors?
- Are you having difficulty paying bills and successfully completing other life tasks because of your behaviors?
- Do the people you associate with spend their time together taking drugs, sexing, drinking, and gambling?

If this has made you think that you would benefit from talking to someone, please contact Warren Broad at 1-(705) 224-HELP or at hello@warrenrbroad.com. All medications and medical issues should be supervised by your family doctor.

Warren Broad is a licensed hypnotherapist with many years' experience in assisting people to make their lives better. Always striving for new and innovative solutions to issues as unique as the people who share them with him, Warren strives to create an environment of caring, privacy and discretion which frees people to safely explore their own issues, connect with a unique person who plays many roles, of therapist, friend, and coach. Initial contact is always free.

Beverly Garland

Beverly Garland is on a mission to inspire others who share the dream to make the world a happier place. She has formal training as a Life Coach, Avatar® Master, and Agile ScrumMaster. She gained 18 years of "cat herding" experience managing teams in the computer game industry, and provided career coaching and resume services to executives. When not making artwork, she helps students worldwide live more compassionately via the Avatar Course, and provides private coaching and workshops to help creative people achieve goals gracefully.

(Avatar® is a registered trademark of Star's Edge, Inc. All rights reserved.)

Contact Beverly at:

www.thelifeholistic.wordpress.com

Skype: BeverlyGarland

bgarlandcoaching@gmail.com

facebook.com/TheLifeHolistic

twitter.com/bgarland

pinterest.com/lovelyplanet

linkedin.com/in/beverlygarland

CHAPTER 26

PRODUCTIVITY FOR CREATIVE PROCRASTINATORS

Beverly Garland

The seeds of wonderful expressions of art, invention, service and social change lie within us, and within those around us. Sadly, even the most humble of these projects will remain hidden from the world as long as the bearer of that seed does not take action. When people can't make progress on an important goal, they often name procrastination as one of their stumbling blocks. Some even create additional blocks, like emergency "fires" and busywork, to mask or justify their procrastination. Why would someone hold themselves back this way? And how can coaching help? This chapter covers how I help clients handle two kinds of barriers to productivity—one that occurs when he or she is pursuing the wrong goal for him or her (and procrastination is actually a good thing), and one that comes when he or she is pursuing the right goal for him or her (and procrastination is in the way).

To be productive is a natural human urge, especially for creative types. We love to see our best ideas come to fruition. We like adding value to the world. We enjoy the journey of creating something that was not there before, and stretching ourselves mentally, physically, and emotionally to meet the challenge. Many even regard it as a path of spiritual growth.

Some also associate productivity with concepts that take some joy out of it, e.g., Spartan work ethics, back-breaking quotas, and overtime. It becomes the opposite of creativity and playfulness. "Want-tos" turn into "shoulds." When they also use it as a measure of self-worth based on rigid cultural ideas of success and failure, it is little wonder that creative people find themselves stymied by procrastination.

Because "productivity" has become a bad word, they fight against an imaginary oppressor every time they buckle down to get some work done. Because they might experience the shame of failure, they hit virtual roadblocks of fear when they attempt something they've never tried before. For lack of a better way to manage their inner conflict, they procrastinate.

Procrastination means putting off something intentionally for later, sometimes habitually. It implies an unwillingness to tackle something right now that you feel you should do, or want to do. Are you actually procrastinating, though, or is it something else? One of my jobs as a coach is to watch out for broad assumptions that would lead us off track, and to make sure we tackle the real issue. I look for clues in the conversation that indicate whether my client is dragging his heels because something doesn't feel right about the activity or goal he intended to pursue, or if he is genuinely procrastinating and acting against his own forward progress. Knowing the difference is the first key to correcting course.

Sometimes a client will avoid a task because it just doesn't feel "right." Perhaps she's resisting action toward a goal that's not leading to what her heart truly wants. An example of this would be procrastinating on a boring project that she took on just for the income and stability, at the expense of pursuing a project that would have been more exciting, but didn't pay as much. Stability and money were important priorities once, but they're not feeding her spirit now. Another example would be procrastinating on household organization projects intended to make her home look like something out of a magazine, so her family will be as happy as the perfect neighbors next door. If what her heart really wants is to be more present and connected with her family, following her neighbor's path won't lead her there.

Criticizing herself for procrastinating on a goal or path that is not authentic for the client creates needless suffering, especially if she sticks doggedly to it. In her case, procrastination is an indication that the she needs to re-evaluate the "why" behind her goal, and make adjustments. Some powerful questions for uncovering the authentic "why" would be, "What is so important about the task or goal you are putting off? What would it give you?" Then using the answer(s) to the previous questions, I would ask, "If you had more courage, resources and/or confidence, what would you do differently to achieve [that thing that is so important]?" Digging deeper and exploring new viewpoints this way will help the client get real about what she truly wants. From there she can make the appropriate changes and line up her goals with her new purpose.

Then there is the client who hesitates on the path to a goal because it IS leading to what she truly wants! For instance, she gathers all the information she needs to work on her idea for a new business proposal, but never gets any further. She just can't get around to the next step because of her busy schedule checking emails, playing internet games, pinning decorating ideas to her online vision board, lying exhausted on the couch, and watching all six seasons of her favorite TV series for the third time. There is nothing wrong with doing any of these things, except that she is using them to avoid working on her goal!

People procrastinate the worst when beginning new projects, especially life-changing goals like taking on a project for an important new client, writing a book or play, earning a degree, training for a half-marathon, or switching careers. They can't get started. The very idea triggers fears of success, of failure, of change, and/or of the unknown. Every time they think about it, feelings of overwhelm and intimidation overtake them, and they retreat to what is familiar and "comfy" — busy-work, play, and/or addictions.

I find several approaches are effective for getting the client past this barrier.

First and most importantly, I help her find (or remember) her authentic inspiration for pursuing the goal. I ask questions such as "How will you and others benefit if you undertake this project?" "How will it feel to have accomplished it?" Feeling inspired makes a huge difference! If she can get more excited about the journey to her goal than she is anxious about the unknowns and obstacles, she can use that excitement to bolster her courage. From then on, she can tap into this inspiration whenever she needs motivation.

Second, I help the client reframe any viewpoints that interfere with forward movement. If there is a distraction like family conflict or disorganization, I'll help her explore ways to handle it. If something doesn't go as planned and she gets caught in negativity, I can help her shift to a new perspective.

Third, I lead the client through a process to minimize the unknowns and to reduce overwhelm. I help her break the goal down into smaller milestones, and then coach her to break the milestones down into smaller tasks. I also guide her to consider the following questions. "What is actually involved in carrying this out all the way?" "What areas need more research?" "What resources do you have available?" "How much time per week can you set aside to spend on this project, given your other priorities?" The more real data she has, the less distorted and out-of-proportion the project will seem in her mind. When things are put in their proper, non-scary perspective, it reduces the urge to procrastinate and retreat into busy-work.

From there, she can further reduce the chances of procrastinating by using strategies to make the actual work as enjoyable as possible. The secret to a good strategy is to work with the client's natural way of "doing." For instance, if she gets bored or distracted easily, she may benefit from a work schedule that has permission to "slack off" built in. A great method is to work in 20 to 25 minute intervals with a timer. When the timer goes off, she gets to do whatever else she wants—go outside, look at Facebook, hug someone—for five full minutes before returning to the task. If she needs lots of social interaction, we'll brainstorm ways to include talking to other people in her project. If she has a lot of deskwork to do, but loves the outdoors, we'll explore ways for her to feel more connected to nature while she's working. The more the work seems like "play" and the less it seems like drudgery, the better for productivity!

Wonderful things happen when a client gets on track with his or her authentic goals, and addresses procrastination with effective strategies. He or she starts to enjoy creating again. Deadlines get met. The seeds of ideas blossom into beautiful expressions for the world to enjoy. Of course there are many more flavors of procrastination, and many other strategies besides the ones discussed above. However, the core approach is the same for most clients: Get in touch with his or her inspiration and excitement, reframe the negative perceptions, minimize the scary unknowns, and make working fun. A few powerful questions could be all it takes!

Elizabeth Pennington

Elizabeth is a certified life coach and member of the International Coaching Federation (ICF). She received her basic, intermediate and advance coaching certificates from the school of Coaching Cognition and is a coach on Coaching Cognition's platform. Elizabeth has also trained to become an internet marketer at Marketing Merge/School of Online Business.

Elizabeth has always strived to support others both personal and professional, when introduced to the world of coaching she knew right away she had found her next journey in life, become a life coach.

Elizabeth and her husband Ronnie live in the beautiful state of Kentucky, USA.

www.coachingcognition.com/ElizabethPennington

www.theagetolearn.com

Skype: elizabeth.ann.pennington

facebook.com/elizabeth.a.pennington.3

twitter.com/ElizAnnPenn

CHAPTER 27

CULTIVATING SELF-CONFIDENCE, ONE SEED AT A TIME

Elizabeth Pennington

Self-confidence is knowing your strengths and weaknesses, believing in yourself, having the ability to adapt quickly to unexpected situations and not being afraid of failure.

As a life coach and mentor, I have had many opportunities to work with clients seeking to attain self-confidence.

A client of mine, as a child, was told by his parents he could never play sports of any kind; as a teenager he was told he would never be able to hold a job, and would "never amount to anything." The client's self-confidence was damaged to the point that he felt worthless and that he was a failure. Cultivating confidence one seed at a time, the client has been able to remove the negative beliefs and replace them with positive ones. He holds a full-time job, participates in a sport of his choice and is no longer in fear of stepping out of his comfort zone.

Culling seeds of failure

1. Think of five things where you have failed and write them down.

2. Write down a reason for each of these and why you think of them as a failure.

3. Write down ten ways these failures are actually lessons learned.

4. When you think you are failing, make it a habit to stop and ask, "Why am I going here?"

I'm not asking you to become a perfectionist or to be arrogant, but, if you allow negative voices to stop you before giving yourself a chance to be all you can be, it will be a great loss to our society.

Belief in yourself is far more important than what you think others believe of you. After all, what others believe of you is only their perception based on limited information.

Self-confidence is a state of mind, and needs to be cultivated daily to produce a bountiful harvest of strength, courage and fortitude for a positive attitude.

I had a client that struggled with "fitting in." After our coaching session I asked the client if I could have permission to share his story, with other clients. I assure you the client has given me his blessing; the client realizes his struggles are not unique to him; they also affect thousands and thousands of other people. Also, even though the client gave me permission to share the session, I will not compromise their privacy by using their name.

I'm sure everyone has heard the statement, "They seem comfortable in their own skin." My client felt anything but comfortable in his skin.

The client felt as if people were talking about him behind his back. The client felt this way at work, special functions and even while dining out. The client became so withdrawn he would turn down invitations to not only public events, but family gatherings as well.

The client shared being overweight was his problem and felt embarrassed with his appearance. The client had tried numerous diets; none of them kept the weight off as promised.

During our session I ask the client where he felt the weight problem first started. The client shared, after a few coaching sessions, that it started when he was a child. The client's mother would leave the client with older sibling while she worked. There wasn't much to eat, so if cookies were the only thing in the house then cookies became the meals and the snack. I'm sure you get the picture.

The client also revealed that he and the other sibling, as in many families, had their differences, fought over who was going to get to watch their favorite TV show, etc. The client would turn to food for comfort hence more weight issues.

As the client gained more and more weight, he was picked on and made fun of at school. The client could not participate in sports like the other students, had problems fitting in the classroom chairs, etc. He began to lash out at the other students, only to be punished by the school authorities for causing fights.

As an adult, the client had problems holding a job, which only added fuel to the flames, and, in no way, could the client imagine someone would be interested in him as a date.

This client suffered from the most extreme case of lack of self-confidence. As the client's life coach it was my responsibility to recommend that he seeks professional medical assistance in addition to our coaching sessions.

Over a period of time this client has been able to lose weight and is still working on that issue. He has been going to social functions, attended family events, and has even had a date or two.

I have listed just a few ways the client and I took action to move him from being totally without self-confidence to growing bushels of self-confidence.

- Kept our sessions on time and consistent
- The client completed assignments
- Took breaks during sessions to ease the feeling of stress
- Promised to support each other through the process
- Promised to not give up until the client felt comfortable in his skin

Negative thinking generates many kinds of fears and anxiety, both internally and externally. Negative thinking can come from rejection, criticism, etc. Even though we all have fears to face in some form, for some of us, our fears stop us in our tracks crippling our self-confidence.

Here are a couple assignments I gave the client;

- Planting positive seeds;

    1. Stand in front of a mirror and ask yourself, "Why am I living my life through someone else's eyes?"

    2. Do this every day before leaving for the outside world.

    3. Reframe the negative thoughts:

- Instead of "I can't do this," think "I can achieve anything."

- Instead of " I wonder if she thinks I'm too fat," think " She sees how slim I am becoming."

- Instead of "I'm not worth anything," think "I am worthy and deserve the best."

- Instead of "I am afraid," think " Fear is only in the mind."

- Make a chart with 3 columns

    1. In the first column, make a list of your fears; list no more than 5 at a time.

    2. In the second column beside each fear, write down why you think this is a fear (could be more than one answer).

    3. In the third column beside each fear, write down how you can change the fear into becoming self-confident.

My client shared that he found it helpful to sit in a quiet place and imagine how his life will be as a self-confident person. By creating a positive picture of himself, he gained strength and courage to move closer to his goal.

This client has now become a self-help coach and is reaching out to help others.

During my coaching career, I have asked clients to give me one statement that has inspired them to move forward. Here are some of the answers:

- Make a list of things you have been avoiding, choose one a day and complete it.

- Believe in your intuition and instincts; listen to them.

- Admit you are wrong; take it as a lesson learned and move on.
- Acknowledge your weakness, know that you cannot always be a Super Hero.
- Don't live as a victim, understand that everyone makes mistakes.
- Go out of your comfort zone. For example, if you are timid, try going to more public functions, or maybe volunteer to be a door greeter.

As a life coach and mentor I have had the privilege to work with people from all walks of life. We have walked though all sort of problems, issues and situations. At the end of the day when you have cultivated your self-confidence, one seed at a time, you will have the ability to spread your wings and go from where you are to where you want to be.

Plant your seeds of strength and courage daily. Grow the ability to cultivate your self-confidence.

Carol Metz Murray

Carol Metz Murray is a spiritual entrepreneur, business mentor, consultant and speaker. She teaches entrepreneurs how to organize and implement strategies, get stuff done and make money. Carol lives her purpose by being the change she wants to see in the world and removing limitations to her personal growth, through constant opportunities for self-actualization. Her leadership background of over 20 years with business, non-profits and government provides her with extremely diverse and rich experiences. Carol is passionate about helping women entrepreneurs find their voice to live the life that is rightly theirs.

Contact her at:

www.carolmetzmurray.com

www.nakedleadershipinc.com

Skype: carol.metz8

facebook.com/busempowerment

twitter.com/c_metz

linkedin.com/pub/carol-metz-murray

CHAPTER 28

YOUR UNIQUE LEADER'S VOICE. A JOURNEY THROUGH TRAUMA

Carol Metz Murray

What's the greatest opportunity in your life right now? What's preventing you from getting it?

Imagine! This is the story you just shared with me.

Momentarily your life flashes before your eyes, as you fly through the air tightly secured inside your car. Your airborne takeoff is like a 747 lumbering down a runway. You realized that you've just hit "black ice," driving a tad too fast, the invisible kind that pulls you in like a funnel cloud.

You prayed. You felt the bitter cold winter wind bite across your face. It was kind of cool flying through the air. Coming in for the landing, snow surrounded and blanketed you. You hung upside down with fuel leaking everywhere and the car engine still humming. Terror filled your soul.

You wondered if anyone would really hear you screaming because you were down the side of a mountain lying in eight feet of snow. Silence was everywhere. You pushed yourself through the hole that once was the windshield, and you pushed and pushed more, to climb through the snow. You suddenly remembered to check to see if you're still alive. You wondered why your eyes weren't focusing. It was almost eerily peaceful right at that moment because there was nothing you could do. Then you noticed your vocal chords were frozen, paralyzed in time. Fear gripped your body and your soul. You wondered what had become of your unique expression of who you are.

As a mentor working with clients, I have discovered that every trauma visible or invisible helped shape their life, making them into the person they are today. Life can be quirky sometimes. You just never know when unexpected twists and turns, bumps and pot holes, deep gullies or wide valleys will blow sand in your face. Each situation is unique. I've asked coaching clients, "Have you ever been there and felt that you've tried to make a positive change yet continually fail?" Could be that you're struggling to change a behavior that is inconsistent with your inner unique voice, with your values and the authentic you.

Have you ever felt knocked down, unheard, dismissed? Have there been lingering doubts about what's not happening, even though you've felt you were making every attempt to do so? The shock of the situation keeps you moving forward. Yet, silence is everywhere. In life, it's not how many times you get hit, it's how often you choose to get back up on your feet. At that moment a deep sense of peace overtakes you. Deep inside of you in the midst of trauma something snaps. You know at your core that your silence has been broken.

In that moment, you begin to scream and shout, sob and sing because you know you'll be okay, and you know that your voice will be heard. With a breath of gratitude, you begin the long climb up the mountainside to bring life to your unique voice.

Coaching clients have asked me, "Why should I really care about finding my unique voice, why does it really matter?"

Do you remember? You learned at an early age it was safer to keep your voice at a barely visible hum, and unexpressive. You allowed fears and anxiety to overtake you and run your life. You didn't ask for help; you handled life as it came your way. You were expected to be seen and not heard.

Excruciatingly wonderful, relentlessly gentle!

Finding your voice and telling your story is hard. It takes courage, commitment and energy to move through the fear, letting go of what was and moving toward what is. It takes guts to learn to trust yourself to speak up, step up, step in and lead from the inner core of who you are. But it's the only way to share your mission in life, live your purpose, touch the world and leave a legacy. There is an art to finding your unique voice. Finding your voice is a journey. Amazingly, people support you when you begin, and on through once you're found your voice.

The journey can be painful and raw, yet it allows you to explore the core of who you are, to acquire a deeper, richer understanding of you. As you shed the layers of trauma to begin to uncover the real, authentic self, the naked leader emerges, totally exposed, vulnerable, yet strong. This is building from the Inside Out. Guess what, folks? Taking shortcuts can create havoc and crisis with chances of being traumatized all over. Missed cues, failed starts, blocked out parts, reluctant feedback seekers have the potential to roll over you like a tornado leaving much destruction in their wake.

The million dollar question is, will you commit to the process? Do you have the tenaciousness to face the potholes on your road of life? It can be scary. Get out of your own way; keep going regardless of the "shift" you're going through. I feel your pain; I see your gain. Connect with your values and see your life soar!

Trauma, whether hard or soft, gets stored in the brain stem. The body may learn, at any age, to jump into the fetal position when confronted with a loud noise. It can also learn to undo the learned behavior. The human body experiences encapsulate each trauma and traumatic experience, which can result in your voice becoming paralyzed. Whatever may have been the cause, generally your voice shriveled like a collapsed balloon with its air supply cut off.

Physical traumas heal quicker than the emotional trauma, which your body stores for you like an armor of steel. There are a variety of resources to help you with the physical and emotional traumas, some more extensive than others, like movement. Mixed in with the body healing is the attitude of possibilities. Your adulthood may be filled with physical or emotional trauma, significant injuries, accidents, divorce, family conflict and illness, unresolved childhood trauma, limitations, barriers, death or grief. It's devastating, challenging or an opportunity; but let's be honest, it's what you make of it. You've got choice. You can shrivel into a victim or you can grab hold of its strings until you are creating beautiful music.

When you begin to understand the genealogy of your life, the patterns you chose to model or create, or the beliefs that cocooned the emotional trauma, then you can begin the process of claiming your authentic voice. As a mentor, I ask clients about their experience learning to ride a bike. Every single one of us remembers riding our bike for the first time and what that felt like. Freedom! It's freedom if you pay attention to where you're going. Riding on a country farm road, being inattentive to the surrounding environment like the neighbors' cows grazing, smacking headfirst into a cow, only to find oneself face down in five feet of water, unconscious leaves its mark.

What must you do to give birth to your unique Voice?

When I have worked with clients, some of them have expressed concerns about making changes in their lives, only to find that the changes fall short of the mark. They wonder what's gone wrong. Superficially, you can attempt to shift behavior. It may work for some time, and then you find yourself back at square one. I realized that I could continue to repeat the same patterns or take a different route. Letting go of old behaviors was a great place to start. If I continually exceed the posted speed limit with a value of respect; how am I able to shine my light and be a demonstration for others?

Traumas are like ticks, they tend to secure themselves tightly to the body. If you are wanting to improve your quality of life or your business's quality of life, be prepared to shift and change who you are. It's not about stopping behavior; it's about wanting to expand who you are; about looking for the possibilities in stepping beyond your comfort zone to uncork more of your unique voice. When mentoring business clients, I encourage them to shift their perception; together we move through dance steps that diminish their "buts" to a dull roar. Trauma can be unlearned and moved through dance, and a variety of other movements like yoga or exercise.

As a business empowerment coach I encourage clients to keep moving through the "Shift," regardless of the muck they find themselves in at the moment. The resulting trauma that I experienced from flying through the air and finding myself in eight feet of snow was a huge wakeup call. There I was, with a possibility to take an inventory of my life, to begin to unwrap my unique voice, say goodbye to my fears, one by one; then to be open to mining the naked leader within to allow my unique voice to emerge. Through movement and voice expression, I became a public speaker allowing my light to shine.

No pain, no gain. Be thankful for the hard times; they can only make you stronger. Be thankful for the possibilities; for they can open your heart. Be thankful for your words; for they can change you. Never give up on yourself. Understand the power of your unique voice; allow it to express who you are.

The path of naked leadership is the path of the individual; what goes on inside is reflected on the outside. Eagles are a great metaphor for this ... having watched eagles hunt for their prey, the magnificence is that they keep moving forward in their own perfection. The world will be moved one day by your voice. You have greatness inside of you waiting to be shared. The cost of not following your heart is spending the rest of your life wishing you had. Will you take the step to live the life that is rightly yours?

Peter Frumenti

Peter J. Frumenti III is a Certified Personal Freedom Coach and founder of the *Path to Awesome* community. His mission in life is to help *you* break out of false paradigms to live the adventure. Peter has a unique perspective on living life without limitations, having transformed his life after a bankruptcy, painful divorce and move to the Rocky Mountains. In December 2011 he ran the Honolulu Marathon after losing over 200 pounds, and five days later took his first backpacking adventure 11 miles and several thousand feet in elevation along the Na Pali Coast. He spends his free time hiking, floating, living, loving and laughing!

www.pathtoawesome.com

www.pathtoawesome.com/blog

gplus.to/peterjfrumenti

- **info@pathtoawesome.com**
- **facebook.pathtoawesome.com**
- **youtube.com/makethedecision**
- **twitter.com/peterjfrumenti**
- **pinterest.com/peterfrumenti**

Get access to free tools to help you find your Path to Awesome at www.pathtoawesome.com/tools

CHAPTER 29

FINDING YOUR PATH TO AWESOME: BREAK FREE AND LIVE THE ADVENTURE

Peter Frumenti

I often hear from coaching clients that they feel "insane." "There is another person; a voice that lives inside my head, a voice that tries to boss me around and tell me what to do," they will say. "It tells me to eat that extra piece of pizza when I shouldn't. It tells me to hit the snooze button just a couple more times, and to skip that run I set my alarm extra early for."

In many different ways, people are conditioned to hold certain beliefs. Finding out what conditioning is significant to you is a personal process. It requires you to question why you feel the way you do in any given moment. That voice might tell you that you are bad at math, that your neighbors are shallow or that your siblings should spend their money more wisely. Maybe you have dreamed of starting your own business, and that voice has told you that you aren't the type of person that takes risks or can do something like that. Is this true?

I often hear people say that they don't set goals because they don't want to fail at achieving them. Why is it not okay to fail? Too many people give up after one mistake or failure, disregarding that those who have been most successful in life have failed and picked themselves back up over and over again. Failure is less scary once you have done the internal work and begun to realize that you are here living this life for you, and not to impress or compare yourself to your neighbors, your friends, your family or anyone!

Your life is yours to live if you choose! In order to find your *Path to Awesome*, you must understand where the important choices you make and beliefs you hold come from; so that you can make ones better suited to you. You need to know who you are and ask yourself, "Why do I think what I think?" Reading this book is an opportunity to ask yourself powerful questions, and so I invite you to do just that.

Question every thought, belief and emotion you have. This isn't to suggest you judge these thoughts, beliefs and emotions, but instead that you dig deep and find out why you think the way that you do. What life experiences have brought you here and made you feel this way? Asking this question of yourself is an imperative step in your evolution and the evolution of our world. The change this world needs begins with each individual choosing to understand who they really are.

From the moment you are born, you are like a sponge. When you can spend some time around young children you will be amazed at the habits, mannerisms and emotions they will mimic. A client once shared a story with me about his first time babysitting his sister's children. He recalled how one of his nephews was playing and jumped off the swing, only to land hard on his knee. My client immediately ran over to see that his nephew was okay. The nephew was just staring blankly down at his knee and the new sensation he was experiencing. My client went on to say that when his nephew looked up and saw the concern in his uncle's face, he immediately turned red and began to shake violently, almost as though he was possessed. "It happened in an instant, right before my eyes," my client said. "His reaction was completely based on mine."

You have the power to change how you feel in any situation, to shift your perspective. Coaching clients often remark that even during some of the most difficult and emotionally painful times in their lives, they have found individual moments where they were able to laugh and find joy. This is something I encourage everyone to practice. Even when the world is crashing down around you, and you have screwed up so badly that you can't bear to look anyone in the eyes, it is in these and in every moment that you have an opportunity, a chance to make a choice in how you feel and what you will do next. I frequently get to see the benefit coaching clients have from taking the time to reconcile the past in their efforts to move forward with a new outlook into the future.

The challenge for many as they practice moving forward and shifting their outlook is that an internal change is a shift in perspective that others simply can't see. Often I hear how hard it is to believe in oneself when those around them still see them as a cumulative result of their previous actions and mistakes. To truly have a chance at changing, at building new habits and finding who you are, you will have to break free from the labels others have placed on you—and even more so from the labels you have placed upon yourself. Can you stop worrying what others think?

If you are ready to move forward with your own life plan, you can! If you want to break free and live the many adventures this life has to offer, you have to begin practicing the act of understanding your previous choices. You will need to begin making new ones based on the reality you want to create for yourself, despite what others might choose for you. Below are some steps that I invite you to take, and questions you can ask yourself for each in developing the practice of these new habits:

1. **Start by visualizing what you want**—Every single day. You have to program your brain to believe in the reality you wish to create. Your brain is like a super computer. It will try to balance any equation you enter. If you have convinced your brain that you are a person who makes positive choices and has amazing things in your life, your brain will work to create that reality. In order to start this process you must know what reality you wish to create. As you begin to see it in your mind's eye, it will become clearer to your brain what outcome it is to produce and what actions you will need to take.

   "What do I want my life to look like, feel like, even taste and smell like?"

2. **Practice recognizing your emotions.** Our emotions are a powerful force. As an example, social anxiety is a problem many people face but don't talk about. Working with clients on social anxiety, they explain that they feel a lot of fear and emotion when meeting new people, and that these emotions dictate what they believe others are thinking about them. Others struggle with the ability to stay calm and focused

during critical communications where there may be conflict or high stakes. The first step in changing this is being mindful of your emotions. Over time you can work through these emotions, but first you need to master the practice of recognizing them.

"What emotions arise in me that have held me back in my life?"

3. **Stop Judging people and be kind.** Only recently discovered mirror neurons have allowed us to learn complex social behaviors, many of which formed the foundations of human civilization, as we know it. These mirror neurons have shown that our brain recognizes the sensation of someone else scratching their arm just as though we are scratching our own. Our brains are not able to distinguish the difference between what happens to us and what happens to others. It stands to reason that our brains also can't distinguish between what we feel about others and what we feel about ourselves. If you want to feel better about yourself, to be happy and forgive yourself when you make mistakes, you must do the same for others.

"How can I be more empathetic and understanding of others, and how might this help me do the same for myself?"

4. **Forgive yourself and learn.** Successful people get comfortable with failure because they do it often. Failure is not a sign of weakness unless you don't learn and grow from it. Those who are open to learning and are able to move quickly past failures take advantage of more opportunities; and although they fail more they succeed more as well. If you want to bring big things into your life, prepare yourself for failure and get used to dusting yourself off, getting back up and taking on the next challenge.

"What can I learn from this and what will I do next?"

Creating a life that wakes you up in the morning, excited to face the adventure ahead, is what this life can really be about. If you are ready for something different, you have to do something different. I hope that the words on these pages will convince you to take action and break free. The steps above are a great place to start; the more you read texts like these and surround yourself with others on a similar journey the sooner you will find yourself traveling down your *Path to Awesome...*

Anita Sechesky

A Registered Nurse, Certified Inspirational Life Coach, International Author, Keynote speaker, NLP and LOA Practitioner, Anita studied her Masters in Marketing at the School of Online Business, and is completing her Advanced Life Coach through Coaching Cognition. She is the CEO and Owner of Anita Sechesky – Living Without Limitations. Anita has helped many people from all walks of life break through limiting beliefs in past failures, health, goal setting, self-esteem, leadership, and motivation. She is compiling her 2nd anthology project entitled "Living Without Limitations – 30 Stories to Balance Your Mind, Body & Spirit" to be released in early 2014.

You can contact Anita at the following:

www.anitasechesky.com

Skype: anita.sechesky

- ✉ **asechesky@hotmail.ca**
- 🟢 **facebook.com/AnitaSechesky**
- 🟢 **facebook.com/asechesky**
- 🟢 **twitter.com/nursie4u**
- 🟢 **pinterest.com/anitasechesky**
- 🟢 **ca.linkedin.com/pub/anita-sechesky/3b/111/8b9**

CHAPTER 30

LOVE ... IT'S WHAT YOU'RE WAITING FOR!

Anita Sechesky

Let me tell you, one of the most common trends I hear about is the fear of commitment when I coach people. Many of my clients have expressed this since everything around them is moving at such a rapid pace, and it seems that relationships are expected to move at the same speed. I have coached so many men and women who are struggling with whether they are ready or not for true love. Many times, we get so busy in our lives with routines and responsibilities that we put aside our longing to be accepted and loved by another person. It doesn't matter who you are and what you do for a living, you have every right to love and be loved. Unfortunately because of bad experiences and setbacks in life, both genders are in the same boat when it comes to feeling that they are not worthy or good enough to actually find someone who will care about them and accept them just the way they are.

For example, I hear reports from people that after a few dates, the discussion moves to who's moving in with whom. When this decision is made, the dynamics automatically change. People want to be loved and feel secure. Even those who don't move in together feel pressured; somehow believing they have to act in a certain way. Every relationship needs to be taken genuinely without the strain of being too serious and uncomfortable. Therefore, allow yourself the freedom to be just who you are and let yourselves get to know each other instead of pretending to always be someone else. There are so many people who think they have to prove themselves to others and act differently than they normally would around friends and family. You may even be focused on a certain type of person and then expect them to be similar to someone you used to know. How fair is that to the new people you meet in life? It would be no different from starting a job and then being expected to behave and even perform the way a former employee did.

Individuals tend to associate their status with their popularity. If they are single, there's no priority involved in a relationship, which may become neglected anyway and therefore has to fight for its survival. That being said, any personal connection whether it is a marriage, friendship or dating all need to be a central focus of attention in a person's life or it will become stagnant, sickly and slowly die away. I use these terms of comparison to health. Just like we have to keep our bodies nourished and active by giving it the daily attention it needs to be healthy, the longevity of a partnership with someone needs to be addressed as equally as everything else in one's life.

So now if you are ready to have true love in your life, let me ask you this: do you believe it's possible for you? No matter what topic I coach my clients on, if they do not believe in it whether it is a goal or a dream, it can never happen. What you set your intentions and focus on is what you will get out of it, plain and simple. It all begins within you.

At some point, you will have to come to a place of forgiveness and let go of ALL past memories associated with former soul ties, especially if you just started dating or are a newly-wed. Yes, I did say ALL! We are complex human beings; we tend to become emotionally attached to people, places and things. If we continue to keep all memories of failed and damaged relationships in our back pocket we will always be remembering, reliving and becoming expectant from those memories. By referencing the things that did not work out in the past, we are missing the things that can potentially work out for us now.

Here is a list of concerns expressed by my clients that can affect a personal relationship with someone:

- Fear of being trapped or controlled.
- Fear from past abusive (physical, mental, financial) situations.
- Fear of being alone causing people to be needy or co-dependent.

- Fear of being compared to past partners.
- Fear of not measuring up.
- Fear of being taken advantage of again.
- Fear of having to change for someone.
- Fear of commitment based on health issues.
- Fear of ridicule from family or friends.
- Fear of infidelity.
- Fear of not having equal household and financial responsibilities.
- Fear of the change in family dynamics.
- Lack of motivation.
- Low self-esteem.

Given that most of these concerns are fear based, many of my clients have admitted to me that it really does affect their confidence and self-esteem. When it comes to having a successful love life, any kind of struggle may potentially affect a healthy outcome. Once the fears and limiting beliefs are addressed and dealt with, it becomes easier to attract the attention and satisfaction that they long for. This is where coaching may help individuals learn how to turn many of their negative perspectives into positive ones for a healthy and loving union.

By establishing trust from the initial connection through honesty, you will help to eliminate many fears of the unknown. There should be no apprehension about what the objective of dating really is. For example, do you just want someone to socialize with or are you looking for a life partner? Be upfront and be real. This way, there are no broken hearts and misunderstandings.

So, now that you're ready for love, you know you are not the only one who has had these fears and concerns. You may discover you've got some internal work to do first.

1. If not already addressed, start by clearing out your emotional closet, making room for all the positive and life-enhancing things that you want to welcome in.

2. Go through the steps of forgiveness, which releases all the memories and emotions attached to past relationships.

This will allow you to be focused on what you really want; something new that will compliment and inspire you to bring out the best in you.

Usually at this point, my clients are ready to address the things they have been neglecting that make them who they are. For example, is there something they used to do that made them satisfied and connected to their self? If they have ignored sports, hobbies or interests, there is still a part of them that is unfulfilled. What makes a person so special and unique are the very things that make them happy deep inside.

Now that you have a clear picture of what you really want, you can see that it is possible to even have a goal when it comes to attracting love into your life. When you become focused, your goals become easier to achieve.

Since people cannot be controlled, we have to recognize we can only control and change our own actions and behaviours. For instance, self-esteem is one of the easiest things to change if we can see it that way. Many of my clients quickly understand the connection to first becoming "Love" so that they can attract love into their lives. You see as you go through clearing out your emotional closet, forgiving and releasing old memories both good and bad, your mind becomes void of anything that may have trapped you in the past. You are empowering yourself to become emotionally clear. Now you are ready to receive and give love that is pure and unaffected from anyone or anything else. Congratulations!

The following is an exercise I have used with some of my clients who are ready to meet the "Love" of their lives. Here are some sample questions.

- Write a letter to either God or the Universe explaining in detail what exactly it is that you are looking for in a partner.

- Be specific about their personality; be detailed about their physical traits (How tall is this person? What is their hair colour, length and style?).

- Include their strong points (psychological, intellectual, and physical).
- Talk about your dream life together. Describe what it looks like.
- How old is your ideal partner?
- What kind of career does he/she have?
- Do you want children? How many?
- Where do you want to live?

It all begins with you and your choices that will move you in the right direction. If you feel that you would still like to work on some of the things I have discussed above, please feel free to contact me.

Live your life without the limitations of the past or the fear of things that have not yet happened in future relationships. You deserve the best and life wants to give it all to you as well.

Let's work through your limitations now because you really are ready for true love to find you!

What are YOU waiting for?

Endorsement

Anita came into my life three years ago at an image building workshop. We bonded over catwalk poses and high heels. She was very bubbly, enthusiastic, and knowledgeable. I later found out that day that we shared the same birthday. We hit it off and sparked a friendship of mutual respect, support, and open communication. A few months ago, I felt myself stuck in my personal and professional life. Being in a leadership position most of my life, it is second nature for me to guide others and give them great insight. However, that was missing for me until I met Anita. As a friend and Life Coach, she helped me to break through certain thought patterns, perceptions and limiting beliefs, and encouraged me to try new ones to attract what I wanted and deserved in life. Everyone goes through periods of low self-esteem. As an eager student, I transferred every bit of advice and guidance Anita gave me and applied it right away. I can say with Anita's knowledge, warmth, and nurturing, I was able to make fast positive changes in my life. I am very grateful to Anita. She is truly a gift!

Nikki Clarke
Host/Founder/Producer, Nikki Clarke Show
Author, Singer/Song Writer

197

Afterword

So now that you have read each of these chapters with the intensity and devotion of understanding for what each of my wonderful co-authors have done to make my Vision for this book come to pass, I trust you can now understand and appreciate how I was intent on making you become the center of focus.

I want to encourage each of you to stretch and grow beyond your own personal limitations, my dear readers, as you continue to ponder over and over again the wisdom and dedication poured into these pages.

As you can see, these mentors are accessible and real people just like you and I. Please feel free to reach out and connect with whomever you choose.

The value contained within this book is precious. Just like gold never loses its value, the knowledge these mentors have poured into their chapters is priceless and worthy of review and application into one's daily life.

Now, my question to you is: "What does your life look like?" Are you struggling with keeping your business, company, family or even just yourself together?

As you can see, I have "successfully" managed, mentored and organized a group of 29 amazing and talented professionals in quite a short time frame of 3 months. I want to help you organize and manage your business goals, just like I have done for myself! This is what

I enjoy most about empowering individuals and groups of people and then seeing their productive results! I have learned through experience and my extensive training how people cope effectively by having an organized system that brings balance with results! There is a secret to helping others where you all succeed!

It is not always easy to keep it together whether it be a company, business or people and also to keep things running smoothly while building the life of your dreams.

I understand the frustrations, tears and stress. I want to assist you in making your dreams and goals a reality.

Together we can develop a "Master Plan for your own Success" and along the way eliminate any "Limiting Beliefs" that have been stopping you all this time. You may even be surprised at what you discover! Your passion is where your strength is. My focus is all about bringing your passion to life.

Let's do this! Connect with me and let me mentor and coach you on how you can step into "Living Without Limitations!"

asechesky@hotmail.ca

With much Love and Appreciation,
Anita Sechesky

The End

CPSIA information can be obtained at www.ICGtesting.com
Printed in the USA
LVOW13s2030211213

366250LV00003B/10/P